English Institute
Essays ❦ 1947

English Institute

Essays ⚜ 1947

NEW YORK · COLUMBIA UNIVERSITY PRESS · 1948

Editorial Committee

Preface

THIS VOLUME, sixth in the series published for the English Institute by the Columbia University Press, includes eight papers read at the meeting of the Institute in 1947. Four other papers, comprising the first half of a two-year series on "The Theory of Fiction," are being reserved in the hope that they may be published, with the four to be read in 1948, in a separate volume. The complete program for 1947 is given in an Appendix.

The 1947 meeting, second since the end of hostilities, was held at Columbia University from September 8th through September 12th. By decision of the Supervising Committee, which has been anxious to preserve a spirit of informality and thus to encourage discussion, registrations were limited to 125. Such are the papers here published that one confidently expects the volume to be of interest to a great many more. The Institute owes warm thanks to the contributors—indeed to all the program directors and speakers. And it would be ungrateful not to mention the members who have offered, from the audience, comments unfortunately not recorded.

We wish again to express appreciation to Columbia University, particularly to Mr. Philip Hayden, and to utter a word of thanks to the ever-helpful representatives of the Columbia University Press.

New York   D. A. R., JR.
June, 1948

Contents

x   Contents

APPENDIXES

English Institute
Essays ❦ 1947

Myth as Literature

✼

By RICHARD CHASE

W E CANNOT CONSIDER myth in relation to modern literature for very long without feeling that the term "myth" is too comprehensive to be very usable. I should like to begin, therefore, by trying to limit the meaning of the word, not in an effort to arrive at an absolute definition so much as to suggest a definition useful in literary studies.

We cannot say, then, that any untrue story or idea is a myth. If someone tells us that "the threat of international Russian expansion" is a myth, we know, of course, what he means, whether or not we agree with him. But suppose we phrase it differently. Suppose that instead of "the threat of international Russian expansion" we say "the Red menace." Surely, we feel, however vaguely, that "the Red menace" is *more* mythical than the original phrase. As soon as we perceive this, we feel that the term which tries to describe *both* phrases cannot be very precise. The difference between the two phrases indicates the direction which our definition, as literary scholars, must take. The phrase we intuitively feel to be the more mythical of the two is so because it contains an image (red), because the word "menace" makes us think of something living and terrible, a dragon or a scourge, and because the phrase as a whole is obviously calculated to play strongly upon the passions.

A difference in context and intention may make the same "untrue idea" either more or less mythical. In an economics book the law of supply and demand may be stated flatly and dispassionately as a truth. If we think it is an untruth, we shall do well to call it simply that, and save the term "myth" for the law of supply and demand as it is pictured in a philippic by a member of the National Association of Manufacturers, who translates a barren idea into an image of the All-father or the *élan* of the universe.

As for a story, we cannot suppose that a novelist makes a myth out of the life of Abraham Lincoln simply by changing some of the biographical facts. That would indicate a purely statistical method of defining myth: history becomes myth when a certain number of dates and incidents have been misrepresented.

A second opinion about myth which is only indirectly useful in literary studies belongs primarily to anthropology. I mean the notion that a story or idea understood, admired, or believed by a whole class or a whole society is, *ipso facto,* a myth. A mythical idea, properly so called, *may* be entertained by great numbers of people, may be a cultural image having great normative or aesthetic value. But that is not in itself what makes the idea mythical. The anthropological definition, again, is too broad for students of literature and also, I suspect, for anthropologists. We feel intuitively that the idea of the Empire State building, as it is entertained by millions of Americans, is mythical. But we have to turn from anthropology to psychology to find out why: we have to consider such things as the symbolic value of the building, its color, its shape, its size, and the stories which cluster around it, the number of men killed in its construction, the suicides who leap from the summit—in short to the quality of the emotive response to it. The binomial theorem is understood, admired, and believed by millions of Americans, but that does not make it a mythical idea in the sense that the Empire State building is.

Again, the elusive American idea which we designate by the word "Mom" has the most crucial and pervasive significance in our culture. But before this idea can be properly called mythical, we have at least to notice the different ways in which the idea is presented: differences in the mode of symbolization, differences in context and intention. When the idea of "Mom," which we vaguely feel to be "mythical," appears in art forms, we have something tangible to deal with; we can perhaps determine to what extent and in what ways the idea is mythical. Thus we must look to specific representations of the idea: one of the many movies in which the strong, enduring, wise, and mature woman strokes the worried brow of her regressive, baffled, defeated, and inarticulate lover; or such highly literate novels as Isabel Bolton's *Do I Wake or Sleep* and Robert Penn Warren's *All the King's Men*.

"Mom" is an example of a pervasive cultural image which is also represented mythically in different kinds of literature. My point is that it is this representation

which makes it, in varying ways, mythical. The anthropological notion of myth, as I once discovered in
a controversy with an eminent lady anthropologist,
leaves no place for T. S. Eliot or W. H. Auden. These
poets are known only to a few people: therefore their
poetry is not mythical. No anthropologist has *said* this
as far as I know. But that is the logic of their position.
I do not mean for a moment that the study of cultural
images may not be relevant to the study of literature.
It is highly relevant in the books of Constance Rourke,
for example. I speak here only of the study of myth, a
more limited and special problem than the study of
literature.

A third misleading idea about myth is that any story
or poem which invokes or refers to the remote past
thereby becomes mythical. This idea is based upon the
traditional—but in the light of modern anthropology,
highly erroneous—notion of the "mythical age" of
man. The implication of this idea is that in the early
ages of history all literature, as well as all cognition,
was mythical whereas in our own later ages human
thought has left the mythical stage and become
rational or enlightened, or at least disillusioned. This
idea further implies that a modern poem is mythical
because it refers to Aphrodite or Prometheus. But
these mythical beings, as we know them, are the
creatures of highly rational and sophisticated poets
whose thinking was not necessarily more or less mythical than that of our poets. The Greek poets did not, of
course, make *their* poems mythical by referring to a
yet more ancient mythological literature. Aeschylus'

Prometheus is a primitive and original creature who takes his being *from Aeschylus' poems*. So with Shelley's very different Prometheus. Any personage in any poem must earn the right, so to speak, to be called mythical, and he must do this, regardless of his origin, within the poem in which he appears. Henry James's *The Golden Bowl* does not become mythical because one of the characters is named Adam, nor is *The Waste Land* a mythical poem because it mentions Tiresias.

Stated very generally, the fourth and last idea which I wish to question is that myth is philosophy. We can distinguish two aspects of this idea: (1) that myth is a cognitive activity; a proto-scientific or proto-philosophical attempt to understand natural, social, or metaphysical phenomena; and (2) that myth is not only cognitive but has normative value as dogma and is therefore a world view or a way of life.

The idea that myth is a naive mode of explaining the universe has had currency at least since the time of Thales and Pythagoras who, apparently, thought that the old myths contained secrets about the operations of nature. And this has been the common rationalist opinion right down through the Enlightenment philosophers, the "Aryan" philologists, and the Victorian rationalists to such a modern philosopher as Santayana and such a folklorist as Joseph Campbell. This idea has been opposed by two heroes of mythological study, David Hume and Herbert Spencer, and in later times by Dewey. Their perception that myth is not primarily cognitive (I do not say it has *no* cognitive value) has been abundantly supported by the American anthropologists. Professor Ruth Benedict, for example, finds it "ironic that the academic study of folklore should have labored through its course under the incubus of theories explaining seven-headed monsters and magic swords as survivals of primordial conditions, allegories of the sun and moon or of the sex act or etiological philosophizing and have ignored the unconfined role of the human imagination in the creation of mythology"—a clear challenge, certainly, to literary scholars to take up what is in the nature of things their proper study. But as literary scholars we must be aware that the rationalist fallacy often pervades our own thinking. This has been borne in upon me recently in reading current Melville scholarship, the great majority of which presents Melville as a sort of bumbling philosopher who wrote books in order to discuss the nature of the universe and to arrive at something called "the ultimate truth." This attitude represents a serious underestimation of what creative literature—poetry in the larger sense—is and does.

No doubt there are certain senses in which the word "myth" may justifiably be used to signify a world view, a way of life, or a whole intellectual-emotive cultural synthesis: for example, T. S. Eliot's "Christian society" or the agrarian Utopia on which the Southern writers once took their stand. This vision of the Southern writers, at once archaist and futurist, with its pleasing picture of the man of passion and tragic sense living in an organic society and emulating Cicero and Castiglione and Burke, is certainly in some sense of the word a myth. I think, however, that we ought to call it so only in so far as it may be delineated aesthetically. This will keep us from confusing myth with dogma and theology and religion, which are something else again. To say, as many modern writers of various persuasions do, that we need to discover or manufacture a comprehensive societal "myth" before we can hope to have an admirable culture and a fruitful literature is to make two related errors—the error of placing an impossibly heavy burden on one human faculty (for myth alone will not make a Utopia, any more than reason alone) and the error of putting the cart before the horse: myth proceeds from culture and literature, and not vice versa. This is not to say that myth has no normative moral value. It has. Like other modes of art, it sometimes speaks with definitive moral authority. Myth may even be said, as Malinowski points out, to have the efficacy of dogma; but as that excellent writer makes clear in his *Myth in Primitive Psychology,* myth is made *ad hoc* to sanctify cultural and aesthetic phenomena. Myth is fluid and adaptable —less so than the historical process, but more so than dogma.

The opinions about myth which we have been discussing have one thing in common: they are formalist descriptions. I hope I do not sound like a Soviet Commissar if I say that formalist descriptions of myth—if they are nothing else—are misleading: but that would be true only if I were trying to substitute one formalism for another. As Andrew Lang remarked, the attempt to produce formal descriptions of myth has for centuries been "the history of rash, premature, and exclusive theories." That is why some other attitude toward myth is necessary.

In discussing what myth is not, we have been led to suggest what it is: namely, literature. The question of how myth is related to culture, philosophy, or religion is the question of how literature is related to these things; or rather, it is a special aspect of the larger literary question. And it is a special aspect because myth is a special kind of literature; myth is literature functioning in a special way, achieving special modes of expression. The remaining problem in this paper, then, is to suggest what special kind of literature myth is.

Myth is magic literature, literature which achieves the wonderful, uncanny, or brilliant reality of the magical vision of things. Magic is a compulsive technique for controlling experience and creating or resurrecting the sense of reality. It is a mimetic device, at once utilitarian and aesthetic—indeed it is utilitarian *because* it is aesthetic—for summoning that supernatural force the savages call *mana* and compelling it to do one's bidding. Myth, R. R. Marett has said, is *mana* grown picturesque. In the vision of the magician, objects take on the quality of *mana* in exactly the same way in which they take on other qualities: color, size, sound. This fusion of quality and object produces an impression, not of unreality, but of more than usual reality—an aesthetic reality which impresses the magician as uncanny, awful, brilliant, fearful, or beautiful in its motion or its state of repose.

Magic, we see, is not only a compulsive technique but an aesthetic activity. Magic is immediately available to art and art to magic. Myths may be regarded, on the one hand, as the aesthetic exercise which preserves and reaffirms the magic fusion; myths keep the magician's world—and the poet's world—from falling apart. On the other hand, myths are poetic dramatizations of the conflicts and interactions of powers operating within the qualities and objects with which these powers seem to be identical. If these observations are sound, any narrative or poem which reaffirms the dynamism and vibrancy of the world, which fortifies the ego with the impression that there is a magically potent brilliancy or dramatic force in the world, may be called a myth.

Let me suggest certain modes which the mythical vision of things may take in modern literature—with the thought in mind that the method of studying myth in an American or British poet may be, more nearly than we usually think, the same as that of studying myth in a Polynesian or Algonquin or Greek poet. Of the writers I mention—Wordsworth, Auden, and Yeats—the first may seem to be in strange company. But to speak of Wordsworth in connection with these more modern writers is to remind ourselves of those necessities of poetry which are implicit in poetic composition regardless of time and change.

In a paper read before the English Institute in 1941, Lionel Trilling subjected Wordsworth's "Ode: Intimations of Immortality" to a very illuminating analysis. Trilling's point was that in the "Ode" Wordsworth "is talking about something common to us all, the development of the sense of reality." I should like to turn briefly to Wordsworth's "Resolution and Independence" and show that this poem, too, is about the sense of reality. The usual notion about this poem seems to be that Wordsworth, as poets will, has become despondent. He is lonesome and so poor that he must postpone his marriage, and he fears that the poet's lot is to know a measure of "gladness" in his youth and to sink but too soon into "madness." A walk over the moors, however, and an encounter with a noble and resolute old Leech-gatherer restore his self-confidence and his inspiration. But let us look more closely at the poem. Trilling speaks of the passage on pre-existence in the "Ode" as "a very serious conceit . . . intended to give high value to . . . natural experience." There is such a conceit, or myth, in "Resolution and Independence," and it serves just the same purpose.

Wordsworth's poem is not an exercise in Romantic melancholy. As the poet walks out on a beautiful, bright morning, he is, to be sure, oppressed with his worldly condition: his "solitude," his "distress," his "poverty." But I do not think these words indicate the full content of his despondency:

> as it sometimes chanceth, from the might
> Of joy in minds that can no further go,
> As high as we have mounted in delight
> In our dejection do we sink as low;
> To me that morning did it happen so;
> And fears and fancies thick upon me came;
> Dim sadness—and blind thoughts, I knew not,
> nor could name.

Notice that Wordsworth is talking of "minds"; his sadness is "dim"; thoughts are "blind." In a later stanza we hear that he is "perplexed," and in writing about his poem Wordsworth says specifically that what he gains from meeting the Leech-gatherer is "new insight." The sense of the reality of natural experience, which Wordsworth cherishes above all else, suddenly leaves him. When he speaks of "madness" in an ensuing stanza, he is not using a trope. There is nothing sentimental or soft in the word. He means insanity: the abyss opens before him. The two following stanzas demonstrate the dilemma Wordsworth is in:

> Even as these blissful creatures do I fare;
> Far from the world I walk, and from all care;
> But there may come another day to me—
> Solitude, pain of heart, distress, and poverty.
>
> My whole life I have lived in pleasant thought,
> As if life's business were a summer mood;
> As if all needful things would come unsought
> To genial faith, still rich in genial good;
> But how can he expect that others should
> Build for him, sow for him, and at his call
> Love him, who for himself will take no heed at all?

Now, these lines are, to be sure, full of apprehension concerning the poet's worldly estate and full of self-blame. But what is responsible for "the fear that kills," the sudden wave of "fears and fancies," that has come over the poet? Is it not that he perceives a scale of values other than his own and that he suddenly fears that the other scale is the true reality and that if this is so, he is lost in an appalling emptiness? Wordsworth's sense of reality, the whole foundation of his sanity and productiveness, is called into question. For the moment a rival reality presents itself. The word "resolution" in the title of the poem does not mean anything ethical like "the determination to carry on." It means, I think, the resolution of a dilemma, the banishment of a false reality, the reassertion of a true reality. And the true reality is reasserted mythically.

The old Leech-gatherer appears to Wordsworth as a revelation. It is so felicitous a revelation that it seems to have happened out of the necessity of Wordsworth's dilemma. The appearance of the old man may be "a leading from above, a something given." The reason why the Leech-gatherer affects Wordsworth so strongly is that, as we should say, he has *mana*. He is a rough-hewn man of flesh and blood, but he is also a vehicle of natural forces and a visitor from the primeval world ("like a man from some far region sent"). As Malinowski might put it, he is "a primeval, greater and more relevant reality by which the present life, fates and activities of mankind are determined."

> As a huge stone is sometimes seen to lie
> Couched on the bald top of an eminence;
> Wonder to all who do the same espy,
> By what means it could thither come, and whence;
> So that it seems a thing endued with sense:
> Like a sea-beast crawled forth, that on a shelf
> Of rock or sand reposeth, there to sun itself . . .

I think it important that Wordsworth attributes to the Leech-gatherer just that sense of the reality of

nature which the poet himself fears that he may have
lost. The Leech-gatherer, with his "yet-vivid eyes," is
able to "con" the ponds and pools of water "as if he
had been reading in a book." And Wordsworth
describes the old man's mind as "firm."

Yet the poet does not recover his own sense of natural reality by observing the old man and emulating
him. The vision in which the old man appears (for it
is a vision) is to Wordsworth the essence of reality.
The universe acquires vibrancy and vitality; things
are set in motion again by the presence of the Leech-
gatherer. "Natural experience," which had for a moment become flat and cold, again acquires a "high
value."

I mention Auden's poem called "Voltaire at Fer-
ney" partly because it so unpretentious. It is perhaps
too easy to confuse myth with size, violence, or flam-
boyance. The first four stanzas of Auden's poem are
somewhat loose and discursive; they are almost light
verse. We see Voltaire as an old man returning to his
estate. Approaching his estate, he observes an exile
making watches; he looks at a hospital being built; an
"agent" pauses to tell him that some orchard trees are
progressing well. He thinks of his enemies in Paris,
who whisper that he is wicked. He muses that, like
gardening, the fight against the false and the unfair is
always a worthy fight. And he utters the hortatory
word "Civilize." The fourth stanza is wry, witty, and
final in its judgments: he

never doubted, like D'Alembert, that he would win:
Only Pascal was a great enemy, the rest

Were rats already poisoned; there was much, though, to be
    done,
And only himself to count upon.
Dear Diderot was dull but did his best;
Rousseau, he'd always known, would blubber and give in.

Now a poem like this, so far slack, loose, and discursive, is in danger of "falling apart," of dissipating itself into a kind of vague aura of thought and emotion
which leaves the reader with no total impression. The
last stanza must provide one or more bright and compelling images if a sense of aesthetic fact is to be
achieved—if, in other words, the poet is to recreate the
full emotive intensity of Voltaire's thoughts and to
fuse his own emotions and thoughts into a meaningful
totality. The last stanza runs thus:

So, like a sentinel, he could not sleep. The night was
    full of wrong,
Earthquakes and executions. Soon he would be dead,
And still all over Europe stood the horrible nurses
Itching to boil their children. Only his verses
Perhaps could stop them: He must go on working. Over-
    head
The uncomplaining stars composed their lucid song.

(It has suddenly become night, providing a dramati-
cally ironic situation for the master of Enlightenment.) There are three mythical images in this last
stanza: the sentinel, the horrible nurses, and the stars'
lucid song. In the earlier stanzas, Voltaire, looking
over his estate, watching the progress of civilization,
had been merely Voltaire. Now he acquires the magic
virtue of a superhuman figure, a demigod, an awful
symbol watching over the unruly and disastrous con-

tinent. The horrible nurses who itch to boil their children may stand in Auden's mind for many things. They are, for one thing, ordinary human nurses, who, as a poet knows whether or not he has read Freud, entertain certain sadistic feelings about the children they care for. Again, the horrible nurses are the perpetuators of barbaric stories and superstitious folklore which, as Voltaire notes in one of his writings, they whisper into the ears of children, thereby hindering the cause of civilization and mature rationality. Furthermore, the nurses are themselves creatures of the folklore imagination—the witches of European folktales. Finally, the horrible nurses are the nations of Europe who instead of nursing their children up to the level of civilization conspire to kill them by persecution and war. And so the nurses become awful images of violence and death stirring uneasily in the European night.

The purpose of the magician is to summon the magical powers of the universe into his own control. He does this to enforce reality and signance upon a chaotic and meaningless world and, by opposing the magical *mana* to forces which threaten him or his vision of things, to promote a dramatic clash the upshot of which is a resolution of forces into a new harmony. Voltaire, looking into the sky and hearing the lucid song of the stars, becomes this magician. For the implication of the poem is that Voltaire will be able, once he has heard this magic song, to enlist its help. He will be able to fuse this celestial song with his own song—that is, he will be able to heighten the reality and efficacy of his own song in opposition to evil. Notice that the myth in Auden's poem is something which the poem itself strives to become and does become. It is not a ready-made construct or system of symbols or body of dogma on which the poem falls back.

The problem of studying mythical poems which make use of specific, well-known mythical figures or stories is essentially the same as studying those which do not. We must study how the poem becomes mythical within itself, out of its own structural and emotive necessity. Yeats's poem called "Among School Children" makes use of the myth of Leda and the Swan, but the appearance of Leda does not, by itself, make Yeats's poem mythical. The poem begins discursively; the first stanza presents details and arranges properties. It also states a problem, for the sixty-year-old smiling public man (that is, Yeats) who walks through the schoolroom watching the nuns and children has a "question" in his mind. The question of the smiling public man may be something rather obscure, like What is this vague presentiment of excitement and significance which I seem to feel? The poet, apart from the public man, also has a problem: How to discover in the given situation the energy and order of a coherent poetic statement. The poet needs an incandescent focus around which to consolidate and realize his disunified, incipient thoughts and his more or less random emotions. In short, he needs a mythical image. It cannot, of course, be *any* mythical image, but one that is legislated by the given situation and the as

yet half-unconscious poetic intensity into which it
strives to translate itself.

> I dream of a Ledaean body, bent
> Above a sinking fire, a tale that she
> Told of a harsh reproof, or trivial event
> That changed some childish day to tragedy—

Now the Ledaean body probably refers to Yeats's be-
loved revolutionary, Maud Gonne, whom the poet
was in the habit of representing in various mythological guises. She seems to signify in "Among School
Children" what Leda signifies in Yeats's sonnet called
"Leda and the Swan." The sonnet refers to Leda's
ravishment by Zeus and says in effect that Zeus makes
Leda into a vessel of magic efficacy: she has "put on"
the "power" of Zeus and perhaps his "knowledge"
(as the 13th line of the sonnet alleges), just as the
primitive magician puts on the power and knowledge
of the superhuman forces he invokes. Furthermore,
by a kind of sexual-apocalyptic vision, she has been
made to symbolize a turning-point in the history of
man, an awful revolution:

> A shudder in the loins engenders there
> The broken wall, the burning roof and tower
> And Agamemnon dead.[1]

As Yeats thinks of the Ledaean body, in "Among
School Children," "our two natures," as he says,
"blend." In other words, the poet has now himself become the magician, for he has fused into the develop-
ing process of his poem the mythical force and meaning of Leda, who is, of course, not simply a Greek

[1] See *A Vision,* Bk. V, for the further significance of Leda.

maiden but a complex of images sieved through the soul of Yeats. The invocation of Leda has made the poem possible by bringing the poet the conviction that a "childish day" may be "tragedy"; the uncreated situation presented by the public man in the school-room now becomes significant in such a way that it is available to poetry. Again, the poet looks around at the children, sees in each one a "daughter of the swan," and senses the working of the passions which the myth has inaugurated and directed:

> And thereupon my heart is driven wild:
> She stands before me as a living child.

From there on the poem moves toward its wonderful conclusion out of the necessity of the mood and meaning created by the myth.

I am well aware that to some of my readers my account of myth will seem an impoverishment rather than an enrichment. I have mentioned Dewey. And "Dewey" means a prosaic and arid sensibility, unaware of the further reaches of human experience. I should, however, prefer to call my approach "aesthetic" or "naturalistic" rather than "pragmatic." And I would ask those who do find this "aesthetic" approach an impoverishment if they are not committing a cardinal error of our time: that underestimation and misunderstanding of art which denies it a primary function and efficacy in human thought by making it always dependent on something else, such as theology, dogma, religion, cultural Utopias, the State, economics. Mr. T. S. Eliot, in his famous review of *Ulysses,* wrote that "the mythical method" might make "the

modern world possible for art." This implies that
myth is something else than art, something anterior
to art which operates not within art but upon the
world in such a way that art may come into being. It
implies that artists should be sociologists or theologians or prophets or pontiffs and that art will some-
how issue forth automatically once the proper cultural context has been created. The same idea is expressed by Mr. Mark Schorer, who, writing of Blake,
says that "myth is the indispensable substructure of
poetry." Modern writers have very consciously striven
to create a mythological literature, an attempt which
for various reasons we must think admirable and hopeful. And so if I reverse these dicta on myth I do not
wish to imply any lack of hope for a mythological
literature or any underestimation of its possible
grandeur. We ought to question Eliot and Schorer,
however, and ask ourselves whether it is not better to
say that "the mythical method" *can make art possible
for the modern world* and that *poetry is the indispensable substructure of myth*. When we construct our
cultural Utopia and man it with priests, pontiffs,
commissars, yogis, censors, and the common man let
us not forget to include the artist-magician, who has
always had such a prominent part in flourishing cul-
tures.

My account of myth is not a complete systematic. It
must leave to others the discussion of myth in terms
of anthropology or of literary-philosophical structure,
or of rhetoric, symbol, or semantic. These disciplines
are, of course, necessary. To prove this, we have only to

reflect that myth for sophisticated minds must have cultural, philosophical, and symbolic meaning. Obviously we cannot and should not think of Oedipus, Joseph of Egypt, Philoctetes, or Captain Ahab without thinking of their philosophic, symbolic, religious, or political value. The method of studying myth which I have set forth is not comprehensive enough to lead to a completely adequate definition. What I have tried to do is rescue the word "myth" from the far too comprehensive meanings associated with it in current literary criticism. My definition of myth is, then, only the first step. The second step will have to arrive at a definition which is more comprehensive without being more vague or confusing. But this second step, it seems to me, necessarily presupposes the first.

The Modern Myth
of the Modern Myth

※

By DONALD A. STAUFFER

A FABLE, said La Fontaine, is "a lie that tells the truth." I should like to define "myth" in similar terms of rough justice. The myth, as I conceive it, tends toward a lie at least to the extent that it is not verifiable in science or history. And it tells the truth to the extent that people *believe* that it tells the truth. As Julius Caesar said, "Most people believe what they want to believe." The myth helps them in their beliefs. It satisfies a desire or a need. It answers a riddle. It gives us a home, so that the universe is no longer so dizzying, or frightful, or empty. When we are looking toward a quarter of the sky for a constellation that will orient us in our wandering, there, in the center of our field of vision, glimmers the shadow shape of myth, faint stars that seem to form a pattern, and for a moment we know that we are not lost.

Goethe has said that for modern times, the subject for great art is the portrayal of the soul of man. Let us accept this idea for a moment, and also conceive of myth as something that gives man through a fiction a clearer knowledge of himself, or a belief that he possesses such knowledge. Then we might also accept

Salvador de Madariaga's statement that the great modern myths are to be found in the persons and actions of such figures as Don Juan, Hamlet, and Don Quixote. Here are aspects of the human spirit given such a complete life of their own, so widely familiar— we may even say so widely believed in—that each of us knows himself better in the reckless, or melancholic, or quixotic mood because of acquaintance with these mythical creations.

But in what sense do we believe in Don Juan? Is he any more than a joint heritage of the European community, a convenient clotheshorse on which, borrowed from Mozart's modifications, George Bernard Shaw can hang his own ideas in the dream scene of *Man and Superman?* And tomorrow might we not see a movie called *Don Juan in Hollywood,* with no more belief in its subject, or indignation at the violation of belief, than such a movie would probably imply?

The question which I am obviously raising is the embarrassing question of the relation of art and belief. The common sense answer, that no one mistakes the imagined world for the historical world, was long ago given by Dr. Johnson when he demolished the credibility of the theater: "It is false [he said] that any representation is mistaken for reality; that any dramatic fable in its *materiality* was ever credible, or for a single moment was ever credited."

Yet if we do not credit the fable, how can it affect us? Critics from Aristotle and Longinus down to very recent times have felt that art does and should move us to action, in which term might be included what

I. A. Richards calls "attitudes" and what I would prefer to call moral beliefs that lead toward action. How
can we be moved by something we don't believe in?
When Theodore Roosevelt used to present his argument for the necessity of war by asking: "What would
you do if someone struck your wife?" the necessity for
physical action depended upon one's belief in the
reality of one's wife. But if I asked you: "What would
you do if someone struck Hamlet?" I would have
framed a question that most of us could agree upon as
ridiculous. We are back at Dr. Johnson's dictum that
no dramatic fable in its materiality was ever credited.

Let us make another start. Assumptions which we
act upon instinctively are based on beliefs. Therefore,
if we study our assumptions and actions, we may be
able to assess our beliefs, though they vary from tepid-
ity to fanaticism, and though they are in themselves
intangible. In the physical world, the law of gravity
is intangible. Yet all of us assume that the effects of
disregarding it would be tangible enough. So heartily
do we believe in it that none of us will start for a stroll
by stepping out of a third-story window. What hap-
pens when we consider our assumptions, not in the
physical but the moral world? I doubt if any one of us
assumes that he is in danger of being shot or stabbed
to death by his neighbor. It is possible, though it seems
to me improbable, that we refrain from murder because of the social penalties. Those of us who refrain
from murder because we believe that God gave Moses
on the mount the Ten Commandments are living in
a vital myth. And those of us who, upon analyzing our

more irreligious minds, decide that we refrain from murder perhaps because of the presence of an inner law—a kind of handy check that operates for the sake of preserving the species—are also acting upon a belief, usually unanalyzed and undoubtedly harder to state or even to agree upon precisely because it has no story, no myth, to cling to.

After this expatiation among beliefs and skepticisms and climates of opinion, it is time to set some bounds to our subject. Let us define myth for the purposes of speculation and of getting on with the argument. A myth is a story which cannot with any success be reasonably accredited, but which is accepted without reasoning to such an extent that people act upon its assumptions. Under this definition, a person living within a myth is not aware of its mythical nature. As soon as he consciously thinks of it as something made up, or invented, or codified by custom, it has ceased to be a live myth and has become a curiosity, or a superstition, or a deliberate fiction. As long as the myth remains living, we live within it instinctively.

S. Thompson in his *The Folktale* writes: "Of all the words used to distinguish the classes of prose narrative, myth is the most confusing. The difficulty is that it has been discussed too long and that it has been used in too many different senses." In Professor Thompson's eyes, however, myth implies "a world supposed to have preceded the present order. It tells of sacred beings and of semi-divine heroes and of the origins of all things, usually thru the agency of these sacred beings. Myths are intimately connected with religious beliefs and practices of the people." They are "given religious significance." [1]

Does this conception make myth sound so far-away and long-ago that there is no possibility of us enlightened moderns possessing any myths? I believe not. I would accept Mr. Thompson's definition, and would lay stress upon three points: (1) that myths do not deal directly with the present order—since the present order affords too great a chance of incipient myth being proved and thus becoming history, or disproved and thus becoming a hoax; (2) that myths deal with sacred beings or at least with supermortals; and (3) that myths are connected with beliefs—religious beliefs, if you will. In my own terms, a myth is living only while we live within it, accepting it without question.

I believe I can illustrate what I mean simply and easily. In talking about the possibility of modern myths with an intelligent woman, I speculated concerning whether we had created in America a myth of Abraham Lincoln. I was careful to say that I realized Lincoln was an historical character, but that I believed we had made him something more than mortal, that to the average American Abraham Lincoln, single-handed, tragically and humorously smiling, had freed the slaves and preserved the Union, dying sacrificially, a one-man hecatomb, the fulcrum of American history and the symbol of the United States. My explanation

[1] *The Folktale* (New York, The Dryden Press, 1946), p. 9. Reprinted by permission of the publishers.

did not protect me: my friend was indignant. In her eyes, to call Lincoln a myth was almost blasphemous: it was a vile attack—more vile because indirect—on his humility, on his great sense of brotherhood, on his passion for human equality. I inquired, in some embarrassment, whether any mere human being could fulfill in his mere mortal life all the functions that popular American history has demanded of Lincoln. Her answer was: "Yes! Lincoln did!" I submit that my friend was living in a living myth. Since I am living in the myth, too, I am not going to waste time in the nefarious attempt to show that Lincoln popularly conceived is a "myth" in quotation marks. And the shades of Washington and Jefferson may rest in peace as well. As for Woodrow Wilson and Franklin Roosevelt, they are on their long journey and their backs are towards us; when they turn their faces, transfigured, in some fifty years shall we say, they too may look at us under the aspect of myth.

Yet only out of some such material may we moderns draw our scanty store of genuine myths. The ambient atmosphere of our times allows us to breathe only history. If a man has not lived historically, he cannot be alive. The mustard seed of doubt destroys any structure of myth in the sense in which I am using this word. That is why Davy Crockett has more chance of being an American myth than Davy Jones; that is why Paul Revere and his galloping horse is a better subject than Paul Bunyan and his blue ox. It is possible to accept Shelley's dictum that the great imaginative creators are "the mirrors of the gigantic shadows which futurity casts upon the present" and to build on this dictum a fanciful mythology that shows the American soul expressing its desires—perhaps its future—in bright fantasies. It would be an interesting gallery, from Captain Ahab to Paul Bunyan; it would draw on the movies and the comic strips and would include Charlie Chaplin and Bill Hart and Mickey Mouse and Li'l Abner and Mauldin's G.I.'s and the Timid Soul and Terry and the Pirates and Buck Rogers—and above all Superman with his mastery of space and matter and his simple virtue coupled with absolute physical power. But this is not scientific enough to suit us today. It is based too largely on what might have happened or what may happen; it is the soul of America dreaming on things to come—which is a waste of time until they get here. We are a hopeful people, but we are also from Missouri: we believe in the future, but we will believe in it even more when we can see it.

I seem to be cutting down on the possibilities for a modern myth. It cannot exist in the future and elicit widespread belief; it cannot exist too far back in the past because there is not enough certainty then that it really happened, *wie es eigentlich gewesen.* (Many of us would turn Christians more easily if there were evidence to show that the apple Eve ate was a genuine Grimes Golden or Bellflower.) We need for our myths actors doing great deeds in some period which we can accept as historical.

Yet we are further handicapped because we believe in the natural, not the supernatural; and we do not believe that many men have been capable of great deeds. That in itself would be super-natural. We subscribe to the idea of the liberty of the individual, but we prefer that he exercise that liberty in being just like all the rest of us.

The modern myth-maker is confronted by a dilemma: democracy and science have opened up two great *fields* for mythology, in which belief is almost omnipresent; at the same time democracy and science have dwarfed the importance of the human actors without which a myth, in our definition, cannot truly take on flesh. If our definition were not so disconcertingly rigid—that a myth should tell a story with human actors—it would be easier to conceive of modern myths. For in the larger terms of a *conception* commonly accepted and believed in without proof, we have today two great myths: the myth of science and the myth of the state. The myth of science makes us trust the world of matter, because it is subject to the controlled observation of specialists; but it takes away from us trust in ourselves, except when we are operating as scientists. We believe in matter and motion, and we shall believe in our minds when they too have been charted as electrical impulses in the laboratory. We believe that we are composed of elements, but we know not what we do. The myth of the atom is popularly accepted, although scientists are not so certain in their description of this fiction as were the theologians of the Middle Ages in ordering the angels. Yet we shall continue to believe in the invisible atom and doubt the invisible angels; we shall disregard the up-

ward movement of the soul, whose nature is the nature
of a wing, and remain content to scrutinize the
Brownian movement in a suspended drop of oil in a
near-vacuum. A doctor today takes care of the health
of the physical body; in earlier times a doctor was a
wise man who understood the health of the soul. I am
not denying that the myth of science works; it could
not work so well today if it had not been popularly accepted and believed in for three hundred years. From
the success with which the assumptions of materialism
have been applied in science derives also in part our
worship of economics. I am arguing that economics
also furnish the grounds for a living myth: if I mentioned the miracle of the loaves and fishes, or the pre-
cept of casting our bread upon the waters, as possible
aids to the millions who are starving in India, the
frivolity of my non-economic approach would rouse
the indignation of every honest citizen. We believe in
economics; we do not believe in miracles or symbolic
parables.

The other great ground for modern myth rears up a
giant more terrible than any Gargantua or Micromé-
gas or Brobdingnagian—the Giant of the State. When
Shakespeare's Menenius, and Plutarch's before him,
told the story of the classes of Rome constituting the
various organs of the body politic, we had an exercise
in fancy. It is no fancy today—it is a living myth. We
are no more than corpuscles in the body politic. We
can see the frightening unimportance of individuals in
the Fascist and Nazi states so recently destroyed, and
sense it, perhaps, in the Communist practice. Yet we

are aware, too, that in acknowledging and combating such creations of political megalomania—effective because the world accepts them so readily—we have ourselves become controlled corpuscles in the body politic to an extent unprecedented in anything that has ever gone by the name of republic or democracy. The sheer brutal size and omnipresence of the state is crowding individual spirit out of the world, which is smaller than we think.

I take it that the English Institute believes in spirit and the individual, or would like to believe in them. Of what significance they are to society is sufficiently evident in the space such a five-day conference as this does not receive in the newspapers. We talk about the spirit and the individual, the necessary grounds for myth in the sense in which I use it; the world today believes in matter and the state. This is the century of the atomic bomb and of socialism. To science each of us is so many percent of phosphorus or of water; to the state each of us is a taxpayer, a maker of x's to indicate a choice on a ballot, a prospective soldier or recipient of government checks. Is this the human material out of which myths may be made?

This, then, is the narrow circle from which I do not think we shall soon escape: a living myth is a story of extraordinary human action which is widely accepted without question; we accept without question only the ideas of science and the state; the ideas of science and the state, since they minimize extraordinary human action, make a living myth almost impossible to conceive. Yet still, in the midst of our despair, we hope.

"Surely some revelation is at hand." To bring it about we consider the possibility, which in my mind is a contradiction in terms, of constructing or inventing myths without belief. That is why I have called this paper "The Modern Myth of the Modern Myth." We are asking for too easy a solution. We are prescribing a quack salve for a deep-rooted disease. Knowing too much and too little psychology, too much and too little sociology, and practically nothing about the manner in which belief operates in art, we are proposing from the heights of our skeptical sophistication a cure for the great modern spiritual vacuum by suggesting that the world be offered some handy, newly concocted modern myths. Who will believe them? On what grounds? And if they are not accepted so deeply that they guide our actions, how do they differ from the daily monotony of realistic novels on the one hand, whose invention is so pallid that they must be protected by guarantees that none of the historical characters in the novel is historical; or on the other from the escapes into fantasy that are either coy and gamesome or hysterical?

A society that possesses myths is a healthy human society. If we did not know this from our own study of history, we could find it out from Arnold Toynbee (whose knowledge is so wide that he like Einstein is a candidate around whom the myths of the twenty-first century might easily grow). Yet myths will not come into being because some convention votes that they are a good thing to have, or because some poet in sudden whim decides to invent them. They will come into being, as they probably have in the past, only out of deep and long-continued passion, crystallized and given shape, perhaps, by some deeply passionate seer-artist, and slowly absorbed into a common culture because they reflect or create profound convictions, and satisfy the impossible desires of that culture.

So far I have advanced the tragically ironical reasons why modern myth-making seems to me difficult if not almost impossible. I shall now want to reverse the field and consider the most serious, the most conscious, and the most nearly successful attempt at such myth-making. But first I should like to give as a coda to this initial section a quick restatement of my essential positions, in words culled here and there from a representative and sensitive contemporary. Only when we realize the difficulty of myth-making today may we properly value our closest approximation to the myth-maker.

Cyril Connolly, a sensitive critic, is living in an unquiet grave with his eyes wide open. He finds today a triple decadence: of language, of society, and of the myth. "Decadence of the myth," he says, "for there is no longer a unifying belief (as in Christianity or in Renaissance Man) to give to a writer a sense of awe, and of awe which he shares with the mass of humanity." Validity of the myth and vigor of belief, as he sees it, are two of the requisites for a work of art. Yet he immediately adds, from his unquiet grave: "The strength of belief in a myth whose validity is diminishing will not produce such great art as the strength of belief in one which is valid, and *none is valid today.*"

He freely acknowledges that the mythoclasts seem always to be right, for our capacity for reverence so easily turns into superstition (or that modern equivalent of superstition, a neurosis). Yet that will not stop man's sense of reverence which, says Mr. Connolly, man continually exudes like a secretion; and reverence tends to turn even the immediate toward myth. In individual history, he says, "The three or four people whom I have loved seem utterly set apart from the others in my life; angelic, ageless creatures, more alive than the living, embalmed perpetually in their all-devouring myth." And in social history, "Lenin, the father figure mummified, replaces the Byzantine Christ."

Myth-making may be not only dangerous, but also a *cowardly* attempt to escape. "Cowardice in living," he writes. "Evasion through comfort, through society, through acquisitiveness, through the book-bed-bath defence system, above all through the past, the flight to the romantic womb of history, into primitive myth-making."

And yet—and yet—in spite of all dangers and difficulties and despairs, the artist, murdering impossibilities, even today has his function. This is Mr. Connolly's text: "Today the function of the artist is to bring imagination to science and science to imagination, where they meet, in the myth." His language here approximates Wordsworth at his most philosophically mythopoeic: "Poetry is the breath and finer spirit of all knowledge; it is the impassioned expression which is in the countenance of all science." Or as Shelley phrases it: "[The poetic faculty] creates new materials of knowledge." And in Shelley's negative statement of the same thing, the obverse of Shelley's coin: "There is no want of knowledge respecting what is wisest and best in morals, government, and political economy, or at least, what is wiser and better than what men now practice and endure. But . . . we want the creative faculty to imagine that which we know."

Shelley's words on the rarity of this creative passionate energy or belief that alone can make great art come close to the memorable phrase of the modern poet, whose career we cannot consider with too great seriousness, and who says: "It is so many years before one can believe enough in what one feels even to know what the feeling is." It is William Butler Yeats speaking. His passion, the unpredictable sallies of his imagination, his piercing philosophical mind, his single dedication to a long and *directed* career as poet, and finally—is it the luck of the Irish?—his genius, make him a safe guide in seeking what may be done in modern times toward the establishment of myth.

He began as a late Pre-Raphaelite idle singer of an empty day. His early imaginative poems are merely desultory wish-fulfillments. Mr. Connolly's flight to the romantic past is almost a gallop in Yeats, when we encounter a poem (1889) called "Anashuya and Vijaya" and find ourselves in "A little Indian temple in the Golden Age." And perhaps the Indian philosopher of another of his early poems believes that God is a moorfowl, or a lotus, or a roebuck, or a peacock, or a combination of all of these. But probably the Indian himself doesn't believe this, and certainly neither Yeats nor the reader. But then, Yeats is young, he is not yet twenty when he writes, this is his first volume of verse, and he knows himself that he is at the "Crossways."

Being a poet, Yeats has an eye for the actual, and an inner eye for the ideal. How combine them in a myth? In the 1890s he tries two roads-of-the-chameleon. One approach is the deliberate creation of all-inclusive symbols. Perhaps under the influence of Shelley's and Spenser's idealism, and of Blake's private cosmos and galvanized symbols, he creates his symbol of the Rose. What is the Rose? "The quality symbolized as The Rose," he writes, "differs from the Intellectual Beauty of Shelley and of Spenser" in that he "imagined it as suffering with man and not as something pursued and seen from afar." Yet he realizes this significance only thirty-two or thirty-three years after the event. In the 1890s the Rose might be the Rose of the World, or of Peace, or of Battle, or the Secret Rose, or the Rose upon the Rood of Time, or the Rose in a Lover's Heart, or a "Red Rose, proud Rose, sad Rose of all my days!" And that is too much to ask of any rose! He might well say with Blake, "Oh Rose, thou art sick!" and abandon—until much later he successfully turns it to a new use—the attempt at myth through arbitrary amorphous symbols.

His second approach to myth is the expected and

normal one. He turns to the past of his race. The attempt is as heroic (and even longer continued) and perhaps as fruitless, as his own Cuchulain battling against the waves with his sword. In his dramas and closet-dramas and poems, from the time he was twenty until he was seventy he worked over with love and admiration and care those great shadowy figures of Aengus the Master of Love, and Fergus and Cuchulain, and Cathleen the daughter of Houlihan, and Oisin and Baile and Aillin, and Forgael, and Deirdre and Queen Maeve. If Yeats is right in his belief that no great passion ever dies, but lives on in the great mind and memory of the world, always endowed with the possibility of breaking out of eternity into particular time and space, then perhaps his strong imaginings have done, or still may do, what he hoped from them: they may give the Irish a sense of pride in their own history, give them semimythical noble ancestors that might make the Irish nation noble as Thebes and Troy made Greece and Rome. Yet many of these creations had to meet the hard test of the theatre, before the eyes of the people whom they were designed to educate. The myths did not convince them; and seeing them unconvinced, Yeats apparently lost his conviction in turn.

I must do some drastic collapsing in talking about Yeats's most obviously mythical subjects, for the obvious things are not the important things in this extraordinary long and vital career at myth-making. He diminished his emphasis on Irish legend when he found that the epic heroes and the fairy hosts of the

Sidhe inhabited a land of shadowy waters, as unreal as Tennyson's Lotus-Eaters or Morris's Earthly Paradise. If his first volume could take as a theme:

> My songs of old earth's dreamy youth . . .
> Dream, dream, for this is also sooth,

he learns, in twenty-five years, to cast away the embroidery of old mythologies:

> For there's more enterprise
> In walking naked.

One road toward greater reality lies among the people—the songs and ballads of the peasants, the superstitions and half-presences of the folk. But Yeats's imagination was never as coy as Barrie's, nor as deliberately cunning as Kipling's, so that he has left us no Peter Pan or Puck of Pook's Hill.

Another road is the hymning of Ireland in her time of greatness in the historical past—in the eighteenth century. His four chivalric horseman are Swift, Berkeley, Goldsmith, and Burke. Yet again, his sense of humor—which is but another aspect of a sense of balance and a sense of reality—protects him from impossible constructions, and only Swift in his hands attains anything like mythical proportions.

These two roads run parallel in another quest: figures invented, or possessing a basis in history, fairly close to present times, who, like the main characters in historical novels, are freely enough imagined to live easily and significantly in their own passions, but who are given reality by actual humble Irish backgrounds. Demonstrable geography and history chain them to the physical world. The argument would run that since Aherne and Robartes can stop on a bridge and talk about Yeats working in his tower, and since Yeats and the tower and the bridge are real, then Aherne and Robartes may also be believed in. Yeats, in divers of his writings, gave his imagination discipline in constructing reality in this careful conjuration of such figures as Michael Robartes, Red Hanrahan, Blind Raftery, and Mary Hynes.

But again, they can hardly be considered myths, for they have no commonly accepted connotations. How many of us would immediately and naturally associate Blind Raftery with art, in Yeats's personal and historical figure of the blind Irish singer and poet? How many would see Mary Hynes as the symbol of the world's beauty?

Along the last road which he chose, Yeats deliberately substituted universally familiar figures for his local loyalties. Helen of Troy replaces Mary Hynes; Homer is more easily understood as a symbol for the artist than is Blind Raftery. Solomon and Sheba, Leda, the Virgin Mary, Saint Veronica—such names figure in the titles of his later poems, and what they stand for, even though Yeats may shape it to his own purposes, may be more easily and commonly understood. To sustain his own unique thought, therefore, Yeats in the end turns to the great myths of Greece, Christianity, and world history.

So far we have been discussing merely the means for myth-making. What are the beliefs that in Yeats's mind were seeking embodiment? They may be summed up simply: the belief in free spirit. As a single extended illustration of the belief in spirit, I need do no more than mention Yeats's fantastic and continuous inquiry into the occult, from Madame Blavatsky and theosophy and Eastern mysticism down to table-tipping, telepathy, and Rosicrucianism. These quixotic and erratic quests form a lifelong declaration that for Yeats the world of matter, or the world of science, or the world of reason, is not enough. Reality for Yeats, even more than for most poets, lies somewhere in the spirit.

As for the *free* spirit, in a world of increasing bondages and pressures and conformities and uniformities, Yeats dedicated himself unswervingly to the freedom of the individual. It is typical of him to write in 1905 (he was thinking of Synge's *Playboy of the Western World*): "We will have a hard fight before we get *the right of every man to see the world in his own way* admitted." In the realms of social ideas and intellectual fashions, he felt it his duty to constitute himself a member of his majesty's loyal opposition, no matter who might be the reigning majesty. He seems at times contemptuous of liberty and democracy. But the liberty he scorned was one of easy privileges, half-formed opinions, and evaded responsibilities. He did not so much disdain the common man and little people as commonness in any man and littleness of soul. His so-called Fascism is but a belief that we must recover from the errors of too much liberty—"the building up of authority, the restoration of discipline, the discovery of a life sufficiently heroic to live without the opium dream" (1924).

This, then, is the goal: the discovery of a life sufficiently heroic. It cannot be found in artificial political unity, "which is the decadence of every civilization." It must be found in the individual human being. And probably it must be found there by the artist. "The arts are, I believe," Yeats writes in 1898, "about to take upon their shoulders the burdens that have fallen from the shoulders of the priests." He knew it was no simple task, nor a popular assignment. And it was a lonely one. Perhaps he felt the truth of what A. C. Benson wrote to him in 1923 when he was awarded the Nobel Prize: "I am sure you differ from all writers of the time in having the best sort of detachment—the detachment from the urgent *present* which ends by bringing an artist, if he is a great artist, into line with the great spirits of the past and future."

At any rate, Yeats can speculate in such terms as these: "The first nation which can possess the three convictions, God, Freedom and Immortality, affirmed by Kant as *free powers,* will control the moral energies of the soul." Yet this is no easy goal, to be reached by conventions, or programs, or acts of the will. Yeats is not satisfied with Eliot's Anglicanism nor with French Neo-Thomism at one end, nor with the Fascist and Bolshevist idea of the state at the other. His belief can be attained neither by any metaphysics nor by any economic theory. "That belief which I call free powers is free because we cannot distinguish between the things believed in and the belief." Here he is speaking in terms of his own distinction between allegory (which is artificial and rational) and symbolism (which is organic and inevitable); and he is speaking almost in the terms of my assumed definition of myth as a story in which we live instinctively and without analysis.

To set up this belief in free powers in which the belief and the powers are indistinguishable, Yeats devotes the great period of his life as a poet—the quarter century preceding 1933—to the construction of a system. As he writes to his father: "Much of your thought resembles mine . . . but mine is part of a religious system more or less logically worked out. A system which will, I hope, interest you as a form of poetry. I find the setting of it in order has helped my verse, has given me a new framework and new patterns. One goes on year after year getting the disorder of one's mind in order, and this is the real impulse to create."

The system, which gives structure to many of his greatest poems, is most fully presented in his book *A Vision*. No philosophy, psychology, and theory of world history has ever been presented in such mathematically perfect geometric form. The artist's eye has glimpsed this vision of formal beauty; but the reader is mistaking the nature of the artist's mind if he takes the form mechanically and literally. He should be warned by Yeats's own statement that the system should interest his father "as a form of *poetry*." And he should remember John Butler Yeats writing to his son: "You [became a poet] because you had convictions of the kind that *could be best expressed in verse,* i.e. convictions that were *desires,* and such as could never be imprisoned in opinions."

Yeats's diagrams of the Great Wheel and the Historical Cones, therefore, his speculations on the twenty-six Phases of the Moon in which human incarnations are possible, and on the Great Year of the Ancients, are all to be taken with a grain of Attic, or Irish, salt. "If you *believe* in magic," as Yeats says in a flash of his chameleon wit, "it ceases to be magical." The road of a poet is no concrete turnpike. It is the road of the chameleon. The poet sets up tentative fictions, until he finds those in which he can believe— or better, until he finds those where the question of belief does not even come up.

A Vision (1924) presents an enthralling study in its delicate balances between fantasy and revelation. Two of its great intuitions are the importance of Desire in human life, and the Duality of Truth. Body seeks soul; soul seeks body; all living qualities desire their opposites, and in fact cannot be understood without them. Solomon yearns toward Sheba, Sheba toward Solomon; and Wisdom without Beauty, Beauty without Wisdom, are meaningless. This is the condition of the world—a world given structure by antitheses and antinomies, a world in which Chance is ever present and Choice is always necessary, a world which, with its returning cycles and revolving diametrically opposed desires, will persist in its great pattern this side eternity, an eternity which will be crowed in when Chance is one with Choice at last.

Yeats has given mysterious power to his symbols—

so that the great Blakean figure of the archer, shooting
her arrow of desire into another dimension from the
flat circle and cycle of history, recurs in the memory.
And the old myths and accepted stories—of Dionysus,
of the Trojan War, of the birth of Christ—are caught
up into a single coherent imaginative pattern of which
we today are a part. The vision is not smaller in scope
than Dante's. It takes as its province all time and all
space. In place of Dante's descending *bolge* in the
Inferno and ascending ledges on the Mount of Purga-
tory, Yeats has created the twenty-eight Phases of the
Moon on a scale where he can group Shakespeare,
Balzac, and Napoleon in one phase, or in another,
Queen Victoria, Galsworthy, and Lady Gregory.

How should the system, the vision, be taken? To
consider its artificiality absurd is not so absurd as to
fail in understanding how the mind of a poet works,
how he inhabits the world of Make-Believe taken in a
literal sense, how he functions as the unacknowledged
legislator of the world, how he creates visions that have
an odd habit of solidifying into reality. He builds a
structure with gossamer, and before we know it, he has
made a bridge across Chaos. The first section of Yeats's
poem "The Second Coming" has become famous because it describes—it has never been better done—the
world of the 1930s. The poem was published in 1921.
Yet since it was principally concerned with looking
forward to the year 2000, and since it shows Yeats's
power of fusing old materials into new myths at its
most intense and most characteristic, its last section
may be quoted in full:

> Surely some revelation is at hand;
> Surely the Second Coming is at hand.
> The Second Coming! Hardly are those words out
> When a vast image out of *Spiritus Mundi*
> Troubles my sight: somewhere in sands of the desert
> A shape with lion body and the head of a man,
> A gaze blank and pitiless as the sun,
> Is moving its slow thighs, while all about it
> Reel shadows of the indignant desert birds.
> The darkness drops again: but now I know
> That twenty centuries of stony sleep
> Were vexed to nightmare by a rocking cradle,
> And what rough beast, its hour come round at last,
> Slouches towards Bethlehem to be born?

The creative poetic power is at work—making from materials available to all those patterns toward which life may move, if only the patterns are seen clearly and believed in. The materials available to all! How much of the nobility with which Yeats has invested his ideals of tradition, of ceremony, of aristocracy, of custom may we assume sprang from Yeats's association with an actual Lady Gregory at an actual Coole Park? How much of the bravery of his mythical heroes came from the veins of the men he knew, the martyrs and the patriots of the Irish rebellion, so that Cuchulain is but a mythical magnification of Pearse and Connolly? The great Rose Tree of Ireland must grow, and must be watered. And yet, said Pearse to Connolly,

> There's nothing but our own red blood
> Can make a right Rose Tree.

Perhaps this is the only source and soil of all myth— our own red blood. And how many of his eagle spirits, his Queen Maeves, his heroes impossibly brave and gay, found their first inceptions in memories of Maud Gonne?—"Angelic, ageless creatures, more alive than the living, embalmed perpetually in their all-devouring myth."

However it was done, the poetic process, mixing memory and desire, continued for fifty years in this one man. And the results, though they celebrate personality and individuality, take on that accessibility to the experience of all men which is an essential attribute of the greatest poetry and of myth.

His Byzantium poems, perhaps his best known, are part of the great myth of cyclical history which is a part of his greater myth of *A Vision*. They are complex and they are personal. Yeats believed in the Great Mind and the Great Memory; he believed that this great mind and great memory could be evoked by symbols. Perhaps they can. At any rate, before we dismiss these poetic symbols and myths of Byzantium, we had better also dismiss Plato's Golden Year. And we must also sweep away as refuse Oswald Spengler and Arnold Toynbee.

I venture to suggest that perhaps Yeats's greatest mythical creation is himself. Living in a world which is frightening principally because it is so limited, so sordidly tied down to a mechanical multitude of tiny facts, so thoroughly small and dry, he broke the Lilliputian threads and stood up in all the dignity of an imaginative artist, to the full height of a man. His short play *The King's Threshold* (1904) creates as its protagonist a rebel poet who will starve on the steps of power rather than submit to mere authority. The King speaks of this hero:

> No fever or sickness. He has chosen death:
> Refusing to eat or drink, that he may bring
> Disgrace upon me; for there is a custom,
> An old and foolish custom, that if a man
> Be wronged, or think that he is wronged, and starve
> Upon another's threshold till he die,
> The common people, for all time to come,
> Will raise a heavy cry against that threshold,
> Even though it be the king's.

Yeats himself chose to make that gesture. Like that of his Countess Cathleen, such lonely sacrifice of self is made, not forgetful of the people, but for their sake. It is therefore possible for one blind reviewer, on Yeats's death, to reprimand him with being so far removed from his times; and for T. S. Eliot to say of him: "he was one of those few whose history is the history of their own time, who are a part of the consciousness of an age which cannot be understood without them." Time alone will tell whether or not through his life Yeats has not also achieved "perfection of the work," and has become, by the imaginative art with which he dramatized himself and his relation to his world, a heartening hero, a myth, for "the common people, for all time to come."

We would not really be able to tell whether Yeats had created any myths, or prepared the ground for possible myths, unless we could get a point for perspective some hundred years, say, in the future. And by that time, since the Second Coming is at hand, it might be too late. If there were more men of Yeats's stature, and bold passion, I would not be so sure that the modern myth is no more than a "modern myth" in the most discouragingly cynical sense. At the very least, we cannot but admire his energy. We cannot but be grateful to him for showing us the fascination of what's difficult, and for affirming the mythological basis of all morality in the line he quotes: "In dreams begins responsibility." And to Yeats, more than to any twentieth-century artist, we owe an immense debt for shooting the golden arrow of desire beyond the bounds and atmosphere of the flat world of society and science. He has almost created, or singlehanded he has almost revived, the myth that individual man is a free spirit.

An Approach to the Poem

By WILLIAM CARLOS WILLIAMS

PRELIMINARY

IT IS DIFFICULT in making a poem to keep the elements separate and simple, simple and at the same time meaningful. The tendency everywhere is to overload the verse with "meaning"—for contrast think of one of Mozart's simpler melodies—to philosophize especially. Or else to seek to mystify and to deal in mystery —dignified to be "metaphysics" in our day. Fine. But let us have our mystery essential and not mixed up with procedure and the understanding of our materials, especially when navigating a new language.

I shall speak to you of the poem as an object, as a thing. To point what I mean I shall tell you a story of an occurrence in the old Daniel Gallery, one of the first galleries in New York dealing exclusively in modern pictures.

One of their salesmen, Allinson Hartepence, a wry, intelligent little man, who knew what he was about, and who this day was alone in the gallery for the moment, happened to find himself in the presence of one of Mr. Daniel's most wealthy customers. This woman, no doubt an estimable person and certainly no mean financial asset to the gallery, was looking at a painting which she liked—and would have bought. There was, however, something about it which disturbed her. She turned to Hartepence:

"What is all this down here in this corner?" she said pointing to a part of the picture.

Hartepence leaned over, inspected the area carefully, and after a little consideration stood back and said to the woman: "That, Madam, I should say, is paint."

To go back for a moment, lest I be misunderstood, let me again consider my title, the title of this paper: *An Approach to the Poem.* Please note what I have said there. *An* approach—not *the* approach. I believe such an approach as I shall sketch for you in some of its aspects is basic but it is not the only approach to the poem. The poem is a thing. Granted. But it is also a container. I am speaking of the thing itself which surpasses, as I shall maintain, what is merely *said* in the poem; the topical matter of which it treats.

Continuing with my title: I am speaking of an approach only. I am trying to emphasize an address, a position taken, toward the poem.

Third, still upon my title, I speak of the *poem,* an address toward the *poem,* not of poetry. Rightly considered there is no such thing as poetry; that is, for the grammarian there is, obviously, such a thing; but the poem precedes such a concept and supersedes it to such an extent that the other (poetry per se) can be positively a barrier to appreciation. Many believe that in some way poetry governs the poem so that it comes to some of us almost as a shock that something called "poetry" may block an appreciation of a new poem.

Finishing with that, and returning to the poem as an object, as a thing, let us ask: What kind of a thing?

It is a thing made up of words and punctuation, that is, words and the spaces between them, as E. E. Cummings has sought to demonstrate.

Now you have heard all sorts of comments upon the work of Gertrude Stein who, by the way, was well educated and intelligent—a forceful individual who wanted very much to be an artist. She wanted, too, to start from the bottom, the basic elements. First she studied the human body, dissected it in all its phases, including the mind—which she studied under Professor James. Having absorbed that, and turning to art as her major interest rather than to medicine or to philosophy, she selected as her primary element upon which to dwell: the word. Words, those small bricks with which we would build the arts—poems in our own category as writers.

During the period of her work, influential and fruitful as it grew to be, Miss Stein's emphasis on the word as an object was one of her most important contributions to contemporary art.

So we have an object made up of words designed to have a certain effect, a rare, an elevated effect, which (apparently) cannot be obtained in any other way. There appears to be no peer to the influential poem unless it be among the other arts; but the poem is more articulate than painting, sculpture, architecture, or even music with which it is most often and erroneously compared.

In a sense, and this is a favorite image with me, it is a small (or large) mechanism or engine, as Saintsbury said, composed of words to do a certain job. May I add here, as a forewarning, that it is an engine that needs continual redesigning in each period of the world so as to increase its capacity in order to refresh the world (if possible) in each period by conceiving the world anew in terms of the arts.

We have come out of this, if what I say is correct, with a rather dry proposal that the poem is made up of elements which have been combined in various ways at various epochs—more or less resembling each other (the combined elements) as poems and having turned out to be a tremendous influence in the world—after the event surely, but there, for all that. (For instance take the Renaissance from Dante onward. It was the rediscovery by Christianity of the Greeks and the Romans as poets, philosophers, dramatists, and sculptors that conditioned the great minds of that epoch, etc., etc.)

How is a work of art important?

You've heard people speak of reality. Wallace Stevens spoke of it in his recent oration at Harvard— I was not there but later read something of what he had to say. The poem is related to reality in that it supersedes the particular, being made up of nothing else, by its *form*. Thus it connects the past with the present; and thus we know we are alive; for seeing particulars all about us, and being instructed by the poem that the past was no different, we get our sense of continuity and the world becomes real to us. PROVIDED that we find ourselves able today to recombine the particulars of the past into the poems as those in the past composed them.

To be men today we must emulate the past (we need not exceed it), WE must take the elements, the particulars (which exist today as they existed then) and combine them *today* in a manner similar to the work of the past—but completely different in form—we must make anew! of old particulars.

And if we cannot do work comparable to theirs, in its differences as in its comprehensiveness, then we cannot say that we, as they were, are alive. Our world is not real to us.

But imagine what we are if we only copy them! Imagine what we are if we are so bound in our minds that we are obsessed by *poetry* and make no poems comparable to those of the past. If we cannot invent anew.

Alfred Stieglitz used to tell an effective story about this. He would say, "If there were two doors and over one was written, 'This way to see God' and over the other, 'This way to hear a lecture about God,' everyone would rush toward the second door—for the implications inherent in entering the first door would be so overwhelming that no one would dare to face them."

Standing before the monumental poems of the past, each different from the other, we sense that they represent—that they formally represent—the record of certain accumulations of human achievements; summations of all that is distinguished in men, the most distinguished, as far as we know, that those various ages produced. But those times came to an end leaving those works of art, those poems in their perfections, like complex shells upon a shore. Men lived in those poems as surely as fish lived in the shells we find among the fossils of the past. But they are not there now.

Those ages, for all their perfections, were limited by their concepts of a world which has been much enlarged for us in our day—enlarged and complicated by the ages of *advanced knowledge which has kept pace* with our survival.

What seems true is that each of these summative ages has presented us with a finished product of great penetration and beauty characteristic of its own age and thoroughly different from the poem of any other period. Formally unique.

Now it is not what these poems say, each in its own manner, that is so very different. The basic difference lies in the form of the poem. The age (through the poet) has created a form which has been characteristic of it. It is as though the age, jealous of its life, unique to itself, has been intolerant of any other form and has wanted to prove its mortal existence by making something—of harsh materials—to live in forever.

I do not mean to speak romantically. I am trying to

avoid all romantic treatment of my theme. All I wish
to point to is that the poem in each case by its *form*
creates the reality of a past age. It is not by what the
poem says that we have the greatness of art. It is by
what the poem has been made to *be* that we recognize it. It is a common experience for young men and
women—today as in Athens or Rome or the Middle
Ages, no doubt, to think and to say, "Oh, if I could
only put into a poem what I feel, the world would
listen."

Those oceanic feelings of well-being, of impending
achievement, are common to us all. Social protest that
burns to be spoken makes us say, "Oh, if only I were a
poet!" Or we can turn it about as many good people
do, "Why isn't *that* a good poem? It speaks piously or
truly what everyone knows to be true. It even rhymes!"
Every newspaper is full of such things.

I know that every college boy or girl who thinks of
such things at all feels that something he or she has
composed is "as good as" much that might be found
in the anthologies—especially some of the modern
anthologies! Their feeling is pure, noble, even distinguished—even more so than would be possible to one
older writing a sonnet!—but their means are weak.
They cannot know that for even a Mozart ages of work
have to be done by generations of sweating predecessors, poets (laborers), before the simplest of expressions can come to flower.

Even Bobby Burns reaped the work done in the
Middle English Period—from the thirteenth century
and earlier—broke up the old fourteener, giving him

his ballad form. It is wise to remember the long progress of English, as its poems demonstrate, from the
Anglo-Saxon rigidities—by *invention* through many
changes of form.

And when this is done, when the form has been completed, when it has at last flowered, it begins at once to
become sclerotic and has to be broken down once more
to the elements—elements, as when English first differed from Latin and Greek; as when Italian grew
from Latin and Dante adopted it, taking certain Si-
cilian shortcuts, I am told, along with the Tuscan to
aid him—the language of the people—and used it for
his masterpieces. The elements were new—opening
new realms of feeling unknown to the earlier languages.

Everything has to be broken down, not cynically,
not without a deep sense of its old dignity, to get at
the essential; the *formal* unit in its purity (that has
been tied into now partially meaningless configurations by old languages); a rebellion on new (refreshed)
formal lines:

We must break down
        the line
        the sentence
to get at the unit of the *measure* in order to build
again.

That is what you see, just that process, in the best of
modern verse today, with a few rare exceptions.

But by this approach, which I am trying to sketch,

WHAT we today, I believe, are trying to do IS not only to *disengage* the elements of the measure but ALSO to seek what we believe is there: *a new measure or a new way of measuring* . . . a poem that will be commensurate with the social, economic world in which we are living as contrasted with the past that will return to us our sense of reality in the poem. It is in many ways a different world from the past calling for different "signs," "terms" of different scope, if we are to make that which was recognizable in the terms of the past recognizable also to us today. We are nosing along a mysterious coast-line and have not yet broached the continent. An attitude toward it is all I am proposing—I should not care to recommend what Cortez did to Mexico.

I speak of an approach to a possible continent, such poems as would signalize a complete break with the past, fit to lay beside the work of the past which they would thus affirm by their newness.

It is precarious territory. Every word used may have sometimes double meanings. Presently someone will ask (himself), "Does he mean that he believes the arts are *useful* or that a poem has a relationship to social usage in any age?"

My reply to that would be that there is the same relationship between the poem and society in any age as exists in painting: the real and the pastiche. And let me introduce to you here a term with which you may not be familiar, the managed poem. Any poem in which the impulse on the part of the poet to unabridged invention is limited by direction outside his

craft is a managed poem. This factor is of course fla-
grant in Russia in the neighboring craft of music. But
we have it almost as patent in our own writing today:
when philosophy or religion or whatever else you care
to dig up *uses* the poem for its purposes or in which
other than invention itself is paramount, the managed
poem will appear. Chemistry offers a good example in
another field.

But the reason this is likely to be bad is that the
interfering agency, using the poem for what it proposes, always wants an already accepted form for its
purposes in order to make itself understood—thus
invention, and so reality, in the poem is made secondary.

In Russia, where a new impulse in governments is
flowing into life, heaven knows what reality in the arts
might not appear to enlighten and enliven the world
if it were not suppressed.

The greatness of Shakespeare's work is made secure
by the sureness we feel in him as nowhere *managed*
by church or state. Why, they can't even tell to this day
whether he was Catholic or Protestant.

You can't blame government (as in Russia), philosophy (as in America), mysticism (as in England), or the
Church generally for trying to capture the arts. My
only admonition to you as writers is, Guard yourselves; I would warn you that all that has little to do
with the poem.

Is it unreasonable to seek a new measure co-mensu-
rate with our age?

How can anyone have the supreme effrontery to believe that what we accomplish can be celebrated in the practiced forms of the past? It cannot be *said* what we are and what we do. It can only be proved by our creation of formal configurations that we *were* and so remain. Take the sonnet. Why the sonnet, a famous, rigidly fixed form? What is the fascination it holds for us aside from its capsule form? It is the attempt to do two things: (1) Share in its cultural acceptance and (2) Attain regularity, a contour that can be sensed easily in the face of so much that is (apparently) chaotic in the form of the poem today.

Take the work of such a distinguished writer as Edna S. V. Millay. The career of a writer which began with "Renaissance" and ended (more or less) with a sonnet sequence is in the sense of this thesis a disaster.

T. S. Eliot seems to recognize this by the absence of sonnets in his work. Ezra Pound, one of our greatest poets, wrote a sonnet every day for a year and at the end of the year destroyed them all.

I believe these things are confirmatory of what I would maintain concerning reality and invention:

Even "Dada" had a moment of reality.

I repeat, it cannot be *said* what we are and what we do. It can only be proved by our creation of formal configurations that we *were* and so remain. This is the work of the poet. This is not a fanciful dream, this is a prime imperative for any people. Nor is any art, thus looked at, a Freudian resort: it is labor. Until your artists have conceived you in your unique and supreme form you can never conceive yourselves, *and have not, in fact, existed.*

And do not believe, I keep repeating, that the form of the age will spontaneously appear; that is, that the great age will just accidentally find the unique representation of itself by our looking at a piece of stainless steel and taking a color representation of it. Nothing could be more fatuous. It is the work, the exhausting work of the artist who (not as a vain type) but by working in the guild, the traditions of his art, as an inheritor of all the skills of the past will MAKE the world today.

The poet must learn (yes, of course) from other past poets how to do his work. Nothing occurs spontaneously. The neophyte must slave to do all but impossible and exacting work about him. The craft, virtuosity (as in Mozart), is basic. But the end must be . . . *invention.*

But to invent we have actually, as the word radical itself intimates, to return to the root. Return to the simpler constructive elements of the line—to shake free from the constrictions that have grown into the line and its stanzaic combinations—and to permit a freer (thought-governed) association of the elements.

All this must perhaps wait, still, on virtuosity—but whether virtuosity follows or does not follow, is one of the penalties of thought: Right as it may be, it may not come to fruit.

Virtuosity is something apart, like a storm in the sky which is apart from the sky itself yet assets it.

And for this, for a new language pregnant with opportunities for formal extension, I believe it would be profitable, most profitable, to push our investigations to the more elementary structures of the line, rather than to let our ideas be trapped by traditional figures whose applications are often outmoded.

Over the years a great bulk of poems has been written with occasionally, every five hundred years or so, a tremendous poem, a plant that covers the world and in its form uniquely summarizes it. When you think how little communication has survived in the world *but* art—and the most articulate parts of that POEMS—you begin to see how important such bursts of new feeling have been caught up in these great epical waves.

What we forget is that there seems to be a waiting; a slow laboring to express a new concept which slowly makes its way *to the threshold of expression* UNTIL it can find a *vehicle,* a form unlike the old, untrammeled by the old (the *good* old manner) to which it is usually BAD, a new invention by the poet to embody it.

We, in our day, are, I think, in mid-career toward some such period.

It is said that I exaggerate the importance of new forms. But new forms (new associations of the elemental particles) open the way to new feelings.

It is the content, not the forms, of the poems that count. Granted.

Unfortunately the mind is such that it cannot feel (or allow feeling its sway) without material means. Poetry is sensual, Milton has told us.

When new forms appear (of course, they do not "appear" but have to be invented), *then* feeling is released for expression . . . uncaged. In fact, feeling that has been *restricted* by old forms and has been limited by their archaism only thus GETS NEW LIFE.

That's what I want to say: we cannot feel until the poet, in the broadest sense, has invented the forms in which we *can* feel. *It is not merely to make a thing* called a poem on a piece of paper that the poet is working.

It is to permit feeling to BE by making a vehicle for it.

In this sense, as the great epochs appear, the poet becomes truly the creator by offering that form which allows *man* of that period *to be*.

But there the matter stops; the established form that was so liberating takes on a new character. As the immediate life passes out of it a stasis occurs within the form: the *best* that *can have been made*.

It exists now in blank verse—impossible for the theatre in our day. Invention is lacking and must be lacking for us in it. Is it likely or even possible that we shall invent anything in the iambic pentameter written as blank verse after Shakespeare? Now I ask you? And after Shakespeare had spent a lifetime on it, besides?

To tell what he did to that form, over a lifetime, following Marlowe, would be an hour's discussion by itself.

It has to be broken down . . . to the last shred. For it is in the form that the thought (superseded by better thought) has become lodged and cannot be got out otherwise: and there it is defended (witlessly).

Once more we must break down the form—the ikon.

It may be said, and is said, that by changing the *thought* the form will change or expand to meet it—as the shape of the machine will change to meet the challenge of the air.

Not at all, unfortunately, for the philosophical, social, religious, and what other expansion of the idea seems perfectly willing to get along with the previously accepted form.

The form will not change to meet the idea but will use the old. The form *must* change, if the physical and the spiritual are to be honestly wed, but it WILL not.

What we have to know is that it must BE changed. The form must *be* changed; and that requires a knowledge of the art, whatever art; in this case, the art of making a modern poem.

Why the necessity, you may still ask? Why not accept the old in its old (its sacred!) configurations and adjust ourselves still to them?

Very well. But remember! It is in the structure of the line that the stasis of the *thought* is lodged.

Let me recapitulate briefly at this point:

The writing of verse is to use words formally.

Poems are distinguished from verse by invention; my particular stress—(including whatever else)—being to say *formal* invention.

The history is that the greatest poems are never formally repetitious (except in detail and not always then). Shakespeare was of a group which captured (and exhausted) the iambic pentameter.

For us there hasn't been a basic formal invention in poetry since the English foot supplanted quantity in the Middle Ages.

Meanwhile the world of thought (of the mind, rather) has gone through countless mutations.

The Poem, formally, has been left behind.

And interests (unnamed—economic, tribal, metaphysical, sociologic—group seizures) perhaps retrograde, recessive at least—have wanted it so, and want it and keep it so—normally!

The *line*—the poetic line—is the seat of this stasis.

Now. We exist as poets (a big word) here, today, and nowhere else. What we dare we dare here, today.

Whatever problems or exhilarations we are to solve or enjoy we are to solve or enjoy here, today.

How are we equipped, here in 1947?
There's the set-up for work.

I think there is only one major lead—I think our one major lead, as Americans, is to educe and exploit the significance of Walt Whitman's formal excursions:

And nothing else!

In America we had and still have an unformed, more or less anonymous language which, among our writers, Whitman was the first to perceive and to act upon with firmness and decision—to break down the old forms. This was the first step in our regeneration, in our formal regeneration. To a large extent, unfortunately, it has been to date, our last.

And let me state at once that though I am stressing the break Whitman instituted with the more established prosody and his value to us because of that, several of his greatest poems are in a more or less conventional mold of great and individual beauty and would be thought of by many as his major contribution to the art. Such masterpieces as—

When lilacs last in the door-yard bloom'd—

and several other well-known poems with their anapestic looseness of feeling are very beautiful but I am emphasizing here another element in his work.

What then did Whitman accomplish? A great variety of things, of course; some of them valuable, some of them of little or no worth—governed by his times. But to limit myself to the scope of this investigation, let me limit my question to this: What was Whitman's formal accomplishment relative to the writing of a poem? To this I should add: And what is its value to us today?

But whatever he did you can't get by his first "barbaric Yawp."

I celebrate myself, and sing myself,
And what I assume you shall assume,
For every atom belonging to me as good belongs to you.

I loafe and invite my soul,
I lean and loafe at my ease observing a spear of summer
grass.

Houses and rooms are full of perfumes, the shelves are
crowded with perfumes,
I breathe the fragrance myself and know it and like it,
The distillation would intoxicate me also, but I shall not
let it.

The atmosphere is not a perfume, it has no taste of the dis-
tillation, it is odorless,
It is for my mouth forever, I am in love with it,
I will go to the bank by the wood and become undisguised
and naked,
I am mad for it to be in contact with me. . . .

Stop this day and night with me and you shall possess the
origin of all poems,
You shall possess the good of the earth and sun, (there are
millions of suns left,)
You shall no longer take things at second or third hand,
nor look through the eyes of the dead, nor feed on
the spectres in books,
You shall not look through my eyes either, nor take things
from me,
You shall listen to all sides and filter them from your self.

I have heard what the talkers were talking, the talk of the
beginning and the end;
But I do not talk of the beginning or the end.

There was never any more inception than there is now,
Nor any more youth or age than there is now,
And will never be any more perfection than there is now,
Nor any more heaven or hell than there is now.

Urge and urge and urge,
Always the procreant urge of the world.

You can't imitate that—as we have tried to do. Because
it is and was meant to be only a beginning which we
were enjoined to carry on to new inventions—because

the secret in it was the same as the secret of a bud that will unfold later into a leaf or flower. It is the cry of a man breaking through the barriers of constraint IN ORDER TO BE ABLE TO SAY *exactly* what was in his mind. The first dominant assertion of the necessity for a new form in America. And by that, as an American, he spoke for the world.

What, then, did Whitman accomplish formally?

Let me prepare my reply by saying that his language, the universal Esperanto he thought he was using, is completely out of date. We have no help there. In fact most of his formal accomplishments are on the negative side; what he did best was to abandon all the staid usages of writing a poem and thus bring the sense to unassociated elements of composition. Notice what I say—unassociated—elements. He abandoned formal associations in the body of the poem with a purpose: to make the line free (as he thought).

Formally his great contribution to us which constitutes our major heritage from him is in the break he instituted with traditional forms of the poem. He returned us to the elements of the art—which he associated more or less successfully in his best work but only in a tentative manner.

In Whitman and for us this is in itself an invention of major importance—like a breath of air in a desert. Its implications (he always said he was only making a beginning) is that we take these nascent elements which he broke free for us and recombine them into forms of the present and the future—as the opportunities of a new language offer.

Invention! A new measure! That is the challenge which distinguishes the poem and the poet of importance in the world. Not until Walt Whitman has any major discovery, any formal invention of any great scope, been offered us.

We still speak of Whitman's "free verse"—and that's as far as we see. But the rationale of his verse, why he had to write a verse of such an order has never been sufficiently clarified. The formal imperative which Whitman faced, to rebegin a literature, disengaging its formal elements from past fixations in order to be able to do so, remains unknown. We hear only of something called "free verse" without perceiving what is implied by that term.

According to the concept which I am presenting there is no such thing as free verse—except as a transitional phase: verse is measure—that is the only permissible term. At least that is my premise in this presentation. Of course since I insist on speaking of "poems" instead of "poetry" and since there are some magnificent poems in free verse, then, naturally, there is such a thing as free verse. Whitman's poems are written in free verse.

But let me put it another way: free verse, poems so designated, are poems that have not been measured, or so I believe, poems to which the ordinary standards of measure have not been found applicable or to which they have not been successfully applied. They are, or represent, I believe, a new association of the prosodic elements in the making (or might be so) or of unrecognized elements waiting for final assessment.

Obviously Whitman was not fully conscious of any such refinement of purpose and did not write his verse with that in mind. He wrote as he felt the measure within himself—freely, but by that he uncovered our later opportunity.

The immediate effect was, naturally, shock. We have Oscar Wilde, in short pants, after his popular reception in Lead City, Nevada, going to visit the Jerseyite at Camden and coming away horrified. Mystified perhaps. I don't doubt it. What could he possibly perceive of a new continent of thought? Of feeling? Of a new formal necessity touching all verse?

Here is Whitman again with a poem that must have been rewritten several times, a poem at first called "Poem of the Proposition of Nakedness" but finally published in 1867 under the new title *Respondez*.

Respondez! Respondez!
(The war is completed—the price is paid—the title is
                    settled beyond recall;)
Let every one answer! let those who sleep be waked! let
                    none evade!
Must we still go on with our affectations and sneaking?
Let me bring this to a close—I pronounce openly for a new
                    distribution of roles;
Let that which stood in front go behind! and let that which
                    was behind advance to the front and speak;
Let murderers, bigots, fools, unclean persons, offer new
                    propositions!
Let the old propositions be postponed!
Let faces and theories be turn'd inside out! let meanings
                    be freely criminal, as well as results!
Let there be no suggestion above the suggestion of drudg-
                    ery!

Let none be pointed toward his destination! (Say! do you
know your destination?)

Let men and women be mock'd with bodies and mock'd
with Souls!

Let the love that waits in them, wait! let it die, or pass still-
born to other spheres!

Let the sympathy that waits in every man, wait! or let it
also pass, a dwarf, to other spheres!

Let contradictions prevail! let one thing contradict another! and let one line of my poems contradict another!

Let the people sprawl with yearning, aimless hands! let
their tongues be broken! let their eyes be discouraged!
let none descend into their hearts with the fresh lus-
ciousness of love!

(Stifled O days! O lands! in every public and private corruption!

Smother'd in thievery, impotence, shamelessness, moun-
tain-high;

Brazen effrontery, scheming, rolling like ocean's waves
around and upon you, O my days! my lands!

For not even those thunderstorms, nor fiercest lightnings
of the war have purified the atmosphere;)

—Let the theory of America still be management, caste,
comparison! (Say! what other theory would
you?)

Let them that distrust birth and death still lead the rest!
(Say! why shall they not lead you?)

Let the crust of hell be neared and trod on! let the days be
darker than the nights! let slumber bring less slumber
than waking time brings!

Let the world never appear to him or her for whom it was
all made!

Let the heart of the young man still exile itself from the
heart of the old man! and let the heart of the old man
be exiled from that of the young man! . . .

Let there be money, business, imports, exports, custom, authority, precedents, pallor, dyspepsia, smut, ignorance, unbelief! . . .

Let the reformers descend from the stands where they are forever bawling! let an idiot or insane person appear on each of the stands!

Let the Asiatic, the African, the European, the American, and the Australian, go armed against the murderous stealthiness of each other! let them sleep armed! let none believe in good will!

Let there be no unfashionable wisdom! let such be scorn'd and derided off from the earth!

Let a floating cloud in the sky—let a wave of the sea—let growing mint, spinach, onions, tomatoes—let these be exhibited as shows, at a great price for admission!

Let all the men of These States stand aside for a few smouchers! let the few seize on what they choose! let the rest gawk, giggle, starve, obey! . . .

Let the she-harlots and he-harlots be prudent! let them dance on while seeming lasts! (O seeming! seeming! seeming!)

Let the preachers recite creeds! let them still teach only what they have been taught!

Let insanity still have charge of sanity! . . .

Let the manhood of man never take steps after itself!

Let it take steps after eunuchs, and after consumptive and genteel persons!

Let the white person again tread the black person under his heel! (Say! which is trodden under heel, after all?)

Let the reflections of the things of the world be studied in mirrors! let the things themselves still continue unstudied!

Let a man seek pleasure everywhere except in himself!

Let a woman seek happiness everywhere except in herself!

(What real happiness have you had one single hour
through your whole life?)
Let the limited years of life do nothing for the limitless
years of death! (What do you suppose death will do,
then?)

Returning to my general theme, you can see, following this perspective of my proposals, that neither the
line in any of its variations, stanzaic forms or other
conventional verbal configurations—changing as they
do from period to period, and age to age—have in
themselves any fixed relationship to the poem. All
that can be said of them is that thus we may observe
the usages of the past.

What is not quite so apparent, however, is that
about them the past clings, fixed there past our un-
doing. It is to disengage our own poems from that
web, by so doing most to affirm the past in its magnifi-
cence—but revivified!—that our work should be
directed. Never to imitate. Can the living be imitated
by the dead?

Our language in the United States being somewhat
anonymous, its designation as "English" in common
parlance but especially in our colleges is misleading.
The poem being principally a matter of form it would
be well, once for all, to designate what language we
are using for it here before attempting to make a poem.

Having surmounted that difficulty we should next,
I think, listen to the language in order to discover
what formal elements in it are suitable to our purpose,
syllabic, accentual. Cadence, or whatever evidences

there may be still to invent as relating in it to the English prosodic foot.

Invention would seem to be the next step. Many attempts will be made before our innovations will be fruitful.

Finally something worthy of our language, our history and ourselves may emerge. In the interim every available resource open to us must be investigated— even those, traditional to English, which in the past have most led us astray.

American poems since Whitman have, generally speaking, shown a widespread retreat from his advanced position. It is to be hoped that, with better understanding of our resources, we may in the future profit more than in the past from his great work.

Since Whitman, if what I say is true, the poems written in our circumference may be divided into two categories: those that have regressed from his bold stand and reverted to previous standards—with the prestige natural to such a position—or those that have constantly attempted to recombine the elements of a new verse (which he more envisaged than accomplished), into the poems he wanted to compose.

IT IS THE FORM—(I have tried hard to make this clear)—it is the form which IS the meaning.

And I would have you understand all the irregularities that you find in modern verse—bizarre and puzzling—are attempts or related initiatives toward the discovery (and use) of a new measure.

That is their rationale here as elsewhere in the modern picture (and you can imagine how this will be resisted). But with our history, such seeking, such attempts toward a new measure, are particularly appropriate and, I believe, have an exceptional opportunity to succeed.

I have mentioned the outstanding hero we have produced and tried to evaluate what he did—not so much a hero as a progenitor—to find and to use a new element.

I have tried to show why this is important to us and through us to the world.

We have had a choice: either to stay within the rules of English prosody, an area formed and limited by the English character and marked by tremendous masterwork, or to break out, as Whitman did, more or less unequipped to do more. Either to return to rules, more or less arbitrary in their delimitations, or to go ahead; to invent other forms by using a new measure.

A NEW MEASURE CONSONANT WITH OUR DAY.

Problems Encountered in the Preparation of a Dictionary of American Words and Meanings

※

By M. M. MATHEWS

L ONG BEFORE the completion of the publication of the *Dictionary of American English* in January 1944, those in charge of the University of Chicago Press had considered the problem of keeping such a work abreast of the times. There were several things which made it difficult to arrive at a decision in this matter.

In the first place, the arbitrary adoption of 1900 as the terminal date for the inclusion of words in the *DAE* had doomed the work to a measure of obsoleteness as soon as it was off the press. Then, too, the size of the book, 2,550 pages, made it expensive and otherwise difficult to revise, even if some way could be found to bring the contents up to date. Before publication was finally completed it was likewise obvious to those who had followed closely the preparation and production of the volumes that the material in them was of very uneven importance.

It was felt that the inclusion of words that are old in the language and that have not, in our use of them, taken on any new significations tended to obscure the number and importance of those terms and meanings of terms that originated here. In dealing with such words as *abolish, actress, admeasurement, admire, adventurer, advocate, aftermath, aim,* and a host of others of the same sort, the only treatment that the *DAE* was able to give is quite inferior to that which these words have already received at the hands of the editors of the *Oxford English Dictionary*.

The upshot of the matter was that by the time the final pages of the *DAE* came from the press those in authority had decided to follow it, not with a revised edition, but with a new work altogether. It was felt that the new dictionary should include only those words and meanings of words that originated here in this country. In a work of the kind proposed the most significant material in the *DAE* could be preserved, and other material, particularly that after 1900, could be treated more adequately than in the earlier work. The proposed dictionary, by focusing attention on that part of the vocabulary most likely to interest students and scholars, would, it was hoped, stimulate further interest and research in the American field, thus making possible, from time to time, revisions that would keep it abreast of knowledge in that field.

Inasmuch as I had been on the staff of the *DAE* from the beginning, and had from the outset been keenly interested in the peculiarly American element in that work, I was honored by being asked by the Press to take charge of a staff of quite moderate size and produce a dictionary that would treat in histori-

cal fashion, as competently as is now possible, those
words and those meanings of words that have originated here in the United States.

The problems which I have faced and am still facing
in endeavoring to carry out the intentions of the Press
are of course so multitudinous that I cannot attempt
to enumerate all of them here. I shall call attention to
the more outstanding ones and indicate the efforts I
am making to solve them.

The initial problem, of course, was that of assembling and bringing under control the material available at Chicago for the new undertaking. In addition
to what was printed in the *DAE,* there is in the dictionary room a large amount of unalphabetized material
collected for, but not used in the preparation of, the
DAE, most of this material being of a general nature
and so not falling properly within the scope of that
work. Since this material runs into hundreds of thou-
sands of slips, and since the pickings in it may be
meager, I did not feel justified in taking the time
necessary to examine it exhaustively. Needless to say,
the collectanea should be very carefully sifted, not only
for sorting out any strictly American words and usages
it may contain, but also for the sake of taking out any
material that may be of use to the Dialect Society in its
efforts to round up dialectal and phraseological
material. If plans now being made can be put into
operation, such a sorting can in time be accomplished.

To secure from the *DAE* the material that falls into
the scope of the present undertaking I found it necessary to make a very careful examination. I checked

each entry with the *OED* and with the *English Dialect Dictionary*, as well as with the latest Webster and the Century. I realized of course that this examination was only a preliminary one, and that further scrutiny, both in the editing stage and in the final stages of preparing the new dictionary, would be necessary. To preserve the fruits of my labors I worked from page proof, making jottings about each entry and meaning as I studied it, and marking for inclusion those that appeared to belong in the new work. This preliminary examination required my full time for a little more than six months.

I am placing some emphasis on this preliminary checking because some of my readers are doubtless sufficiently acquainted with the *DAE* to know that those words and senses that are of American origin are plussed. In the "Explanation of Special Lettering and Symbols" in the fore-matter of the dictionary we read, "+ indicates that the word or sense clearly or to all appearance originated within the present limits of the United States." It may therefore appear that so far as the *DAE* was concerned, all that it was necessary for me to do was to appropriate those plussed entries and go my way rejoicing. The reason that shortcut could not be taken was that the pluses in the *DAE* are not to be relied upon implicitly. I do not have time here to go fully into this matter, but I do wish to point out that the system of plussing is especially unreliable in the case of combinative expressions.

For example, *California hat,* included as a main entry, is plussed, but *California blanket* included among attributive uses of *California* is not. Similarly, *California toothpick* is plussed, but *California plan, California horse,* and many other similar expressions are not. Under the entry *Condor* the term *California condor* is included, and plussed, but under the entry *California 2* the same term, *California condor,* is given with no plus indicating the American origin of the expression.

Unfortunately, it was not only in the combinative entries that errors arose in the use of the plus. The most surprising of the erroneously plussed terms are those that occur in the King James version of the Bible, and some of these, possibly, are to be found in earlier translations made use of by the translators who produced the 1611 version. Obviously, the pluses in the *DAE* were of little assistance to me in my efforts to sift out from that work the material suitable for inclusion in the new dictionary.

This first problem of assembling material was by no means finished with the checking I have described. More material, especially from 1900 to the present, was urgently needed. A small amount was already available in the files of the dictionary at Chicago. I went to work as industriously as possible to augment this, reading as widely as I could in modern books, magazines, and newspapers, for new evidence. For a time I subscribed to newspapers from New England, from the South, and from the West, making in this way a feeble effort to cover as much territory as possible. I was able to secure some assistance in collecting modern material from voluntary readers, but a statement may well be made in the Foreword of the forthcoming dictionary that much remains to be done in examining Americana for the purposes of historical lexicography, and that the modern period, especially, will stand much more extensive examination than it has so far received.

The second of my problems was in deciding when a word or a meaning of a word falls into the category of those originating in this country. So far as I know, there is no way in which an infallible judgment can be rendered in the case of every puzzling term and meaning. Of course, a great many Americanisms have been recognized as such for a long time, and about these there is no problem; but there are a great many more that no one can be positive about. At the very outset of my undertaking I considered what policy to pursue with regard to those words and meanings that are questionable. As a rule such terms do not appear in any British dictionary, but it would be foolish indeed to conclude that one is thereby justified in regarding them as of American origin.

In my efforts to deal with this situation, I am proceeding as follows.

1. In entering such words I call attention to the possibility of their having appeared earlier in British use, though evidence for such use is lacking. When it is possible for me to do so, I cite the occurrence of corresponding terms in other of the Germanic languages. I cite these foreign correspondencies, not always to suggest that it was from these sources that we have taken the terms in question, but often to point out

that if the term occurs in Dutch or German, there is a likelihood that it existed in British usage also, though it appears to be absent from the *OED*.

For example, *cook kettle* is recorded as an Americanism in the *OED Supplement,* from which source it was taken over into the *DAE*. Although Horwill in his work on American usage calls attention to the use in America of *cook* in places where British usage would employ *cookery* or *cooking,* I do not feel too positive that *cook kettle* may not be an expression that goes far back in British usage, though for one reason or another it escaped being rounded up for the *OED*. The corresponding expression occurs in Dutch, so I include a reference to that fact by way of suggesting that since Dutch has such an expression, it is at least possible that British English does too, though the evidence for such a term is not at hand.

The question might be raised here as to whether it would not be wise to omit from the dictionary those terms about which I feel doubt. By omitting such terms I could probably increase my score for accuracy, but I feel that omission might harm the cause of scholarship in the future. If such terms are included, the chances for further investigation by those who come after me will be much better than if they are omitted and thus allowed to drop out of the critical observation of later students.

2. I have often appealed to British scholars for an expression of opinion on particular terms, and I have often been pleased by their positiveness on one side or

another with reference to such terms. This coopera-
tion of British scholars will continue to be sought, and
my intentions are to have among those who read proof
on the work a few of those who have hitherto been
asked for opinions on doubtful terms. Absolute accuracy cannot be secured even in a multitude of counsel-
ors, but a closer approximation to it can be achieved
that way.

In deliberating on these questionable terms, I try
to take account of whether the phenomenon denoted
by the word or term is of American or British proveni-
ence. Sometimes this task is as difficult as the original
problem, but by constantly making an effort to arrive
at an intelligent conclusion on this point I sometimes
stumble upon information that may be as welcome
to others as it is to me. For example, a reviewer of some
of the early parts of the *DAE* looked askance at the
entry *Bear-trap* which is plussed in that work. After
pointing out that the formation *bear-trap* is characteristic of the English language and sure to appear whenever one has occasion to set traps for bears, the reviewer concluded: "The compound *bear-trap* is in itself no more American than *mouse-trap*."

The point made by this reviewer may be well taken,
but before one passes final judgment on *bear-trap* he
would do well, it seems to me, to weigh carefully the
fact that the European bear disappeared from England
by the eleventh century. This fact increases considerably the probability that a great many quite common
bear-combinations might actually have arisen in this

country where from the earliest period of colonization to the present moment bears have been in no sense obsolete.

By stressing the problems involved in my work, I hope I do not convey the impression that every single aspect of the undertaking is a problem, and that the finished dictionary will therefore be little better than an exhibition of gropings in a realm where nothing is sure except uncertainty. The fact of course is that hundreds of entries present no great problem at all. In dealing with them I can see my way reasonably clear, but there would be no gain to you or to me in my telling of those things that I feel I am doing pass- ably well. And with this explanation I take up another problem, and one which I think may arouse general interest.

The problem I refer to is that of deciding when a word has taken on a new meaning. Of course in the case of a great many words this is quite easy of solution, but in the case of many others it is hardly likely that scholars would all agree.

In the *DAE* this difficulty of recognizing new mean- ings was not painstakingly faced. Whenever there was a clear indication of the application of the word to a person, thing, or phenomenon that was a part of our American culture, the editors used the plus.

For example, in dealing with the word *chief,* they plussed the first sense or meaning, giving as the defini- tion of the word in this supposedly new sense: "The recognized head, or one of the heads, of an Indian tribe or section of one." A close examination of the significance of *chief* might well, it seems to me, lead anyone to doubt whether its application to an Indian can legitimately be called a new meaning. In the *OED*, s.v. *Chief, sb.* 6. b., we have the following definition: "The head man or ruler of a clan, tribe, or small un-civilized community." The evidence for this sense in the *OED* begins with an example of 1587 that refers to the head man of a Scottish clan. Sifted in with the other examples given in this sense by the *OED* there are some which refer to American Indians, though these examples are not sorted out and placed apart and given separate treatment as should have been done if the editor had regarded *chief* used with reference to an American Indian as having a new meaning.

If *chief* when used of an Indian takes on a new meaning, then it is undoubtedly the case that if it were used to refer to an African, Hottentot, Chinese, or Malayan leader, who occupied a corresponding place in a relatively backward or uncivilized group, the word would successively take on new meanings which unabridged dictionaries aspiring to anything like reasonable completeness would have to take into account. The problems posed by such a procedure are quite staggering to the imagination, and the possi-bilities of similarly multiplied meanings of other terms open up vistas of dictionaries running into hundreds of volumes and being, if producible, quite unpurchasable, and because of their size quite un-usable.

Another good example of the plan followed in the *DAE* is seen in the entry *Blanket,* which is credited with two new American meanings. The definition given of the first of these is: "A blanket belonging to an Indian, and usually worn as a garment." The most superficial examination of such a so-called new meaning is sufficient, it seems to me, to rule it out at once. The fact that a blanket belongs to an Indian who uses it in a somewhat unorthodox manner does not have the slightest effect on the meaning of the word *blanket*. In a way, the editors admit that there has been no change in the meaning of the word, for they define *blanket* by calling it "a blanket."

The second of the so-called new meanings shows the same weakness, and again the word defined is repeated in the definition: "A coarse blanket used to catch the gold dust in gold-washing apparatus." This free and easy way of assigning new meanings to words appears to me to be entirely indefensible. It is hardly necessary to point out that we give no new meaning to the word *blanket* by using a blanket as a garment or as a kind of strainer to catch particles of gold. The only way any word acquires a new meaning, it seems to me, is by being applied to something it has never formerly denoted, and by being thus applied so often and over so long a period that confusion might result from the use of the term in an unmodified context.

Of course I appreciate the difficulty of this problem. There must be among my readers at least a few of those modern semanticists who have a perfectly satisfactory grip on such things as "the meaning of meaning," and who have joyously accepted and can act upon the proposition that no word is ever used twice with the same meaning. I have looked somewhat into the lore of the semanticists on this point, but I have found no comfort. Instead, I have come away from my questings with the feeling of one who has shaken hands vigorously with the east wind.

I have also sought counsel from the best scholars I know, but when confronted with the problems sketched in these paragraphs they have failed me individually and collectively. The most disappointing and upsetting seance I had was with the late Dr. John Matthews Manly. Dr. Manly was of the opinion at the time I talked with him that every word now used in this country, or that has ever been used here, has taken on a meaning quite distinct from that which it has or ever has had in British usage. He cited our common word *the* as having, in his opinion, taken on among us meanings foreign to it in British usage. He was unable to cite any examples of these new meanings, but that inability did not shake his loyalty to his proposition that the meanings are there. After listening to Dr. Manly for a time, I felt disposed to call a carriage and go home and lie down for a while, feeling sure that I should never have mentioned the matter to him in the first place.

This vexing problem of arriving at a practical decision as to when a term has taken on a new sense is not one that can be solved in all cases by any rule of thumb. Each situation must be judged on its merits. It is only in the case of those terms of what may be called "general applicability" that the difficulty of recognizing a new meaning sometimes becomes onerous.

Terms of a relatively specific application, such as *rattlesnake, salt,* and *soda,* also take on new meanings, but these are more easily recognized.

In my search for a solution that will be serviceable to the lexicographer I have inclined strongly in the direction of thinking that terms of general applicability, like *chief,* take on new meanings by being so consistently applied to particular phenomena that by this special reiterated application a definite response on the part of the hearer or reader of such terms can be confidently counted upon whenever the word is used.

Chief is a suitable term for any leader who, in a relatively primitive society or in a tribal organization, occupies a position of leadership and authority. The word does not, for me, carry with it any connotation of race or color, being as applicable to Africans and to Australian bushmen as to Indians or Malayans. No use we have ever made of it in this country with reference to Indians has resulted in the emergence of a definite intellectual response associating it at first blush with Indians. In order to call forth such a response, it must be accompanied by some qualifying term, as an Algonquian chief, Sioux chief, Indian chief, and so on. The same sort of thing, it seems to me, has happened with many other words, but I need not here multiply examples.

On the other hand, the noun *republican* is one applicable to anyone who believes in, supports, or prefers a certain form of government. The term has been used in this country, however, so often to refer to a member of a particular political party that, judged on the basis of the nature of the response which it inevitably causes, it may fairly be said to have taken on a new meaning. If someone tells us that he has been talking with a *republican,* and does not warn us otherwise, we inevitably think that he has been speaking with an affiliate of a particular political party. If he tells us that he has been speaking with a *chief,* we are puzzled until he enlightens us further.

The final solution of this problem of meaning will have to await the arrival of someone who can bring to it more genius than I have at my disposal. The solution which I have ventured is not likely to satisfy all scholars, but it is workable. At any rate, I trust that my efforts to arrive at sensible conclusions by some such means as I have indicated will prove to be of at least some interest.

The next and last problem to be presented here is what I may call "evaluating" the material going into the forthcoming dictionary. This term "evaluating" as I have used it is intended to cover much ground. It certainly involves a consideration of the definitions of the terms that have to be dealt with. Anyone can understand that it is not by any means easy to write proper definitions of some of the words and uses that rightfully find a place in a work devoted to exhibiting in historical fashion all those terms and meanings of terms that have had their origin here in this country.

Every dictionary that I know much about would, if closely examined, reveal instances in which the editors not only nodded but slept soundly. I am sure that remarkable masterpieces of ignorance will be found by my critics in the dictionary under discussion. This problem of definition would of course be much easier of solution if we editors could always know precisely the limits of our own knowledge. We often have to take the word of our predecessors, and if those who went before us are in error it is not always possible to avoid perpetuating their mistakes. Even when we are fortunate enough to feel sure that we are correcting and improving upon the work of those who went before us, we are humbled by the realization that those who come after us will have to perform the same kindly service for us.

The main problem, however, which I desire to discuss under this head of "evaluation" is considerably more subtle than that of definition, as elusive as that often is. As everybody knows, we in this country are, usually, of diverse racial antecedents. If one of my friends tells me that he is descended from French, German, English, or Irish forebears, or from a conglomerate mixture of all these, I would be politely interested, but I would not be surprised. We products of the melting pot are inevitably of complex origins, and the particular ingredients, if I may so express it, incorporated in our existences are not matters of much concern to many of us.

Even scholars, however, have not so far recognized to what an extent the medium of expression that we have developed here on our own soil is likewise a product of the melting pot. Of course, most of us have realized in a general way that our language as we use it in these United States is derived from many sources, but it is not until one seriously sets about this business of examining closely every word and every meaning with which we have enriched our linguistic resources that one makes real and surprising discoveries.

As all of us know, many a foreign word has effected entry into our language in more than one form. As a result of this multiple-entry process we have such related terms as *caitiff, captive; balm, balsam; fay, fate; feat, fact; leal, legal,* and a great many more. There is, however, only an imperfect realization of the extent and manner of acquisition of foreign words here on our native heath, so to speak.

As one studies the evidence so far brought together for such words as *alcalde, avocado, burro,* and many more, it becomes clear that these terms passed into American use, not as a result of previous borrowings made in England, but rather as a result of new borrowings made in this country. The poet Southey used the word *burro* as early as 1800, but the word did not occur in American use until our pioneering forefathers established contact with the Spanish civilization in the Southwest. It is clear that *burro,* so far as our use of it is concerned, is a new borrowing quite distinct from and independent of that made somewhat earlier into British English.

Time after time foreign words and meanings of words have become all but inextricably mixed with words and meanings of what we may call the native English stock, and it requires skilled investigation to unravel the composite result and relate each element in the linguistic situation to its appropriate source.

A few examples of the simpler sort will make the point involved here quite clear. When the first English colonists in New England arrived in this country they found that the Indians of Massachusetts had certain places of defense or refuge. Having no better word for the phenomenon involved, the English-speaking colonists used the old English term *castle* for such an Indian town or fortified place. This use of *castle* did not persist, but the fact that it once existed is important enough to be pointed out.

At about the same time the settlers on Massachusetts Bay were using their English word *castle* in a slightly new sense, the Dutch settlers in New York were likewise discovering that the Indians with whom they came in contact had these towns or fortified places of security. The Dutch, following the same kind of linguistic procedure as was being followed in Massachusetts, examined the resources of their speech for a word suitable for these strongholds among the natives, and they too fixed upon their word *kasteel,* the Dutch cognate of the English *castle.* Those who used English in the New York area converted this Dutch *kasteel* into *castle* and wrote such expressions as: "The Governor . . . by the mistake of his guides hapned to fall short of the castles of the Mauhaukes." Winthrop, over in New England, somewhat earlier told of how "when we came before the town, the castle put forth a flag." Winthrop in using *castle* was using English, but the writer in Albany, New York, in using *castle* was employing Dutch. The dual ancestry of the word *castle* used in these two areas becomes clear to anyone who examines carefully the evidence for the use of the word given in the *DAE.*

A good example of intertwining meanings from diverse sources may be observed in the entry *Sprout* in the *DAE.* The first of these meanings is given as: "A branch or mouth of a river." An examination of the examples—and there are only two of them—to illustrate this use of *sprout* reveals that both refer to the *sprouts* of the Mohawk River. The investigator's suspicions are likely to be at once aroused by this Mohawk background for the only examples of this use of *sprout,* and when the proper steps have been taken to look further into the matter, it is found that in Dutch the word *spruit,* the cognate of the English sprout, is regularly used for the mouth of a stream. With this information, the course of linguistic happenings becomes clear. Before joining the Hudson, the Mohawk River separates into several sprouts or shoots, and it was to these outlets or mouths that the Dutch in that area applied their term *spruit.* English speakers either translated the Dutch term or proceeded at once to their own word *sprout,* on the inspiration afforded them by the Dutch word. The result of what took place is that sense 1 in the *DAE,* s.v. *Sprout,* is an interloper, as it were, stemming from a source quite different from that of the other uses there exhibited, which are senses of the English word. Anyone who speaks of "the sprouts of the Mohawk" is using Dutch, but when he speaks of putting one through *a course of sprouts* he is using English that has been subjected to an American modification.

The same kind of interesting phenomenon is seen in the *DAE* entry *Bed-pan*. Two senses of the expression are given, first that of a warming pan, and in the second place that of a sanitary vessel for use in bed by those who are ill. In the first of these senses, that of a warming pan, the expression is old, but in the second sense, that of a sanitary vessel, there is very meager evidence in the *OED*. The only example given there is one of 1883, but the evidence in the *DAE* of the American use of this expression is as early as 1678. This situation in which the American use of the term antedates that found in Great Britain by two centuries is one that will bear investigation, and this despite the fact that as we all know the dates for the earliest evidence to be found in any historical dictionary are rarely to be relied upon as explicit proof of the first occurrence of a word.

Looking more closely at this early American evidence of the use of *bed-pan* in the sense of a sanitary vessel, we find that it comes from a region of Dutch settlement. And when we turn to the Dutch dictionary and find that in Dutch this same expression, *beddepan*, is used in just this American sense of 1678, we are justified in concluding that the term in this sense was taken up into American use from the Dutch.

Lack of time prevents me from multiplying illustrations of what I mean by "evaluating" such material as is going into the dictionary upon which I am engaged. I cannot refrain, however, from giving one final example, of a slightly different type, that shows admirably how a careful "evaluator" can see much further into a situation than any of his predecessors have been able to do.

In the *DAE* there is an entry *Tabby*, a word defined as: "A concrete made by mixing lime, shells, gravel, and water." In accordance with their usual procedure, the editors of the *DAE* looked to England for the source of this word and this sense. They therefore did not see either in the word or in its sense anything American. True, the earliest British evidence given of the word in this sense is of 1836, some sixty years later than the first American occurrence of the word as shown by the material printed in the *DAE*. But this priority of American over British evidence did not arouse any suspicion on the part of the editors. Nor did the fact that their earliest evidence of *tabby* with reference to concrete comes from the South Carolina area awaken the editors to the desirability of further investigation.

The fact is, or should be, well known that by 1775, the date of the earliest quotation in the *DAE* for *tabby* in this sense of concrete, African slaves had been brought to South Carolina in great numbers. Many of these hewers of wood and drawers of water and mixers of cement were in those days being obtained directly from Africa. Their descendants still live in that region, and are the present-day Gullahs among whom many of the terms handed down to them by their slave ancestors are still in everyday use.

From evidence now available, it is clear that this word *tabby* is one of those brought to South Carolina and Georgia by African slaves in early times. *Tabby* in this sense is not, by origin, an African word but is one of those that in times gone by passed from the speech of Arabs into that of Africans. How the word *tabby* got into British use is of no importance to the student desirous of understanding how the word in this particular sense passed into American currency.

Surely I have said enough, and more than enough, to illustrate clearly the point or problem which I set out to explain about the evaluation of such material. This aspect is perhaps the most difficult of all those involved in the preparation of the work. Correspondingly, the proper solution of such problems as these is that which will most enhance the value of the finished dictionary.

As I have indicated, the procedure I have followed and am following is that of paying the utmost attention to the date of the evidence at my disposal, and also to the area from which the earliest evidence so far obtained comes. In addition, I have schooled myself to avoid thinking in every instance that because a word has existed at some time or other in British English, it was from that source that it passed into American currency.

One who day after day faces such problems as have here been exhibited, solving as many of them as he can, and leaving others in as favorable position as possible for solution at the hands of those who will inevitably come later with far better equipment and skill, is often reminded of the ancient proverb to the effect that "It is the glory of God to conceal a thing: but the honor of kings is to search out a matter."

Problems in the Editing of Shakespeare: Text

By M. A. SHAABER

THE PROBLEMS that arise in editing the text of Shakespeare are many. It is impossible to deal with all of them here, or even with the most important. They are a bit esoteric too. There are possibly not more than thirty men alive (in English-speaking countries) who have edited a play of Shakespeare, and this happy band of brothers is not likely to grow much larger in the near future. I am discussing a highly specialized industry. But if I can illustrate two points that I have in mind—that the proper editing of Shakespeare's text is important, and that it is not inconceivable that in the future we shall be able to make better texts of Shakespeare than we have today—I hope I shall have justified the reader's attention to the matter for a little while.

Although I have said that the proper editing of the text of Shakespeare is important, I hope I may be excused from attempting to define a good text. I believe I could do so, but not in the allotted space. I hope to be let off with a few dogmatic statements on the subject. First, there are good texts and bad—or not so good—texts, and we who study and teach Shakespeare should prefer the good and try to put the good rather than the bad in the hands of those we can influence. This is important because Gresham's law seems to apply to texts of Shakespeare as well as to money: the bad texts threaten to drive out the good. The drugstores used to sell a book advertised to contain the Cambridge text and the Temple notes, as if that were an unbeatable combination. The Cambridge text was an excellent text in 1863 when it was first published; much better texts are available today. But not in the drugstores. I imagine that the best-seller among texts of Shakespeare is and has long been the Oxford. It is not the best text. Besides following some debatable principles, it is, comparatively speaking, full of misprints. The best texts in print are the Neilson and the Kittredge—oddly enough, both American. That they are the best the average reader would never recognize. The difference is not crucial: a bad text of *Hamlet* does not turn *Hamlet* into a bad play. But just because the difference is visible only to an experienced eye and because it is a real difference, we who know the difference should cherish the good and reject the bad.

But the odd thing about editions of Shakespeare is not that they are different but that they are so much alike. They are so much alike that one could say that they all conform to the same editorial standards. How different some editions might be from others may be seen by comparing any of those in print with the specifications laid down for a new edition by McKerrow in his *Prolegomena*.[1] Textually McKerrow's edition is to

---

[1] *Prolegomena for the Oxford Shakespeare, a Study of Editorial Method*, by Ronald B. McKerrow (Oxford, Clarendon Press, 1939).

be as conservative as any, but in matters of editorial practice it often departs widely from what we are accustomed to. It is to reproduce the spelling of the most authoritative early editions. It is to leave the original punctuation unaltered whenever it is not clearly mistaken. It is to keep editorial additions to the text to a minimum: for example, it will not add stage directions unless they are absolutely demanded and it will not add designations of locality at all. Such an edition will be far more different from the Cambridge edition, let us say, than Dover Wilson's or Kittredge's is, radically as these two have sometimes departed from the practice of the Cambridge editors.

I do not know whether McKerrow's projected edition will some day be published; I suspect that the Clarendon Press will not drop the project, but I have no information about it. If it does appear, I believe that it will fill a long-felt want. It will not replace the kind of edition we are accustomed to for what I may call, with no condescension whatever, the ordinary reader, but to many students of Shakespeare's art it will be extremely useful. It might even lead to other editions with somewhat different standards. I shall discuss briefly some ways in which the practice of editors might depart from the established practice to show the possibilities of new and different editions and to suggest how such departures might serve a useful purpose.

There will be no question, I imagine, about the convenience of an edition in the original spelling for certain kinds of study. It is a strange anomaly that, while the standard editions of most Elizabethan au-

thors print the text in the spelling of the contemporary books and manuscripts from which it is derived,
there has never been a complete edition of Shakespeare in the old spelling. One has only to recall how
seriously many peculiarities of Shakespeare's language
have long been disguised by the editions of his plays to
understand the need for a text which does not disguise
them. That it does not disguise many variant and ob-
solescent forms is one reason for specially commend-
ing Kittredge's edition.

Let us consider first the speech prefixes and stage
directions and the designations of acts and scenes—in
other words, everything in the original editions extraneous to the dialogue. The editors have usually
treated this extraneous matter with the greatest freedom, on the assumption, I suppose, that it is even less
likely than the dialogue to be authentic and especially
literally authentic, and also perhaps because tampering with it is at any rate not tampering with poetry.
They have also wished no doubt to give their work a
certain consistency and uniformity lacking in the
early texts. An opposite trend has already set in: Dover
Wilson omits the conventional designations of act and
scene, merely putting the number of each scene in the
margin for purposes of reference; Kittredge preserves
a good deal more of the form of the original stage
directions than other editors and is scrupulous in
bracketing additions to the stage directions and additional stage directions, though he does not indicate
omissions from those of the original editions. The
question is, what is to be gained by reproducing the

extraneous matter with a fidelity equal to that with which an editor tries to reproduce the dialogue? It is a nice question and the answer is not simple. Take the inconsistent speech prefixes of the original texts. Is there any point in designating the same person sometimes as *Nauarre* and sometimes as *King*, as the quarto of *Love's Labour's Lost* does, or sometimes as *Falstaff* and sometimes as *Sir John*? There is certainly no practical advantage. Is there any harm? None that I can see. In a novel the same person is commonly named in different ways. If the author sometimes speaks of him as "Steve," sometimes as "the big fellow," sometimes as "the truck driver," the reader does not seem to be puzzled or discommoded, and I can think of no reason why the reader of a play should not be able to take such variations in his stride. Therefore, since it is pretty well agreed that these irregularities are Shakespeare's work, and since they show him to us absorbed in the process of creation, even though not in a highly interesting phase of the process, a case can be made out for keeping them.

What of the stage directions? The original stage directions are undoubtedly lacking in polish, sometimes in explicitness, and their authenticity has on occasion been suspected. But even if they were not written by Shakespeare, and surely some of them are more likely than not to be his, they were certainly written by somebody closer to his ideas and the practices of his company than Rowe, Capell, or Malone. Moreover, it is quite impossible to understand Shakespeare's stagecraft from the stage directions in a modern edition; any one interested in this phase of the plays must have access to the original stage directions and badly needs an edition which reproduces them. The stage directions also yield important evidence regarding the origin of the text which is largely obscured in most editions. Even in an edition for the ordinary reader it is not altogether clear that there is an advantage in changing "Here the Ladie sings a welsh song" (*1 Henry IV* III. i.247) to "A Welsh song sung by Lady Mortimer" or even in changing "Enter one with letters" (IV.i.12) to "Enter a messenger, with letters."

The question of the act and scene division of the plays is even more vexatious. Everybody knows that it first appeared, in an imperfect form, in the First Folio, and that what we do not owe to the folio we owe to Rowe and later editors. The authenticity of the Folio division is debatable; we do not know how far it corresponds to the practice of Shakespeare's theater. We do know that the division of modern texts is in a few places most misleading where the editors have broken into two scenes what was acted continuously on the Elizabethan stage. Moreover, one need not commit oneself unreservedly to the theory of continuous performance to say that in the text of Shakespeare the word *scene* does not mean the same thing as it does in the present-day theater and that the use of it in the manner of the present day is misleading to most readers. Among others, I believe that the difference is important. On the other hand, at this late date, it would undoubtedly be most inconvenient to discard the whole traditional division of the plays into acts and scenes and with it the conventional mode of locating passages by act, scene, and line, which would make all our reference books useless. It is on the score of convenience alone that McKerrow decides to retain the customary act and scene divisions, though he proposes to number the lines continuously throughout the play as well as in the usual manner. But if Dover Wilson can partly discard act and scene divisions in a modernized text, it certainly seems that editions for initiated students could go at least as far.

For the indications of the place of the action which the editors have foisted upon the plays there is little excuse. Everybody knows that they are completely inauthentic in the sense that there is nothing like them in the original texts, and as they have become sanctified by tradition they range from the obviously correct —as when, finding Romeo with the friar after he has said "Hence will I to my ghostly father's cell," the editors tell us that the scene is "Friar Laurence's cell" (II.iii)—to the downright silly—as when, by labeling the scene "A room in the house of Polonius" (II.i) they imply that Hamlet entered by stealth and stole upstairs to confront Ophelia. All this is really quite unnecessary in any kind of edition. As far as place and time go, Shakespeare's plays are self-explanatory. The editors' statements are of course intended to help the reader, but they do so only because he has learned from modern plays and theater programs to approach a play with certain expectations to which Shakespeare's plays respond only imperfectly. It would be a much greater service to the reader not to encourage this attitude and to throw him back on the plays themselves for the information he needs. If the reader is to conceive the plays as they were imagined by Shakespeare and performed by his fellow actors—and I take it as axiomatic that he should wish to do so—rather than more or less revamped to fit the modern theater, it would be much better not to create false expectations by giving each scene a definite locality. Only then will the reader begin to realize that half the action takes place in unspecified territory and that where it takes place is commonly one of the least important things about it. Only then will the reader begin to form the habit of visualizing the action as taking place on a platform stage rather than in a real place or on a picture stage, and thus learn that Shakespeare's stagecraft unites an almost naive simplicity and directness with great economy and effectiveness. The first step in purging our texts of these unfortunate localizations has been proposed by McKerrow, who would remove them from the text itself and put them in footnotes.

As for the text of the plays proper, I should like to say something about the punctuation and the meter. No present-day editor is likely to adopt the Johnsonian principle of considering the punctuation to lie wholly within his power, and Dover Wilson is notable for the attention which he pays to the original punctuation. Still all editors, Dover Wilson included, substitute their own pointing for the original, whether they have much or little respect for the latter. But McKerrow has said of the original punctuation, especially that of the Folio, "though it is undoubtedly less regular than we are accustomed to nowadays, it really presents no more difficulty than the old spelling does, while it often suggests the way in which a speech is intended to be uttered more clearly than does the more 'logical' punctuation of the modern texts." [2] I believe that he is right, and if he is, obviously it is possible to reproduce much more of the punctuation of the original texts than editors usually do.

The treatment of the metrics of the plays is a most delicate matter. It is an open secret that a good deal of the verse of the early editions is mislined, that is, it is not uniformly printed in units of five stresses. The editors seem to assume that it should have been and they set about conscientiously reforming it accordingly. First of all, as far as possible they conjure verse out of passages printed as prose—sometimes quite rightly, as in Mercutio's speech on Queen Mab, and sometimes very dubiously, as when they try to make Falstaff speak verse. Secondly, when they find two or more successive short lines they try with might and main to combine them into normal lines. Except for the recognizing of verse which the compositor has set up as prose, none of this is very important or helpful. McKerrow has laid down some very sensible rules for treating passages of this kind which I believe all editors would be well advised to follow. [3] But mislineation in speeches of some length is a different matter. Here the editors regularly move words from one line to another, introduce or omit elisions, and exercise ingenu-

2 *Prolegomena*, p. 42.   3 *Op. cit.*, pp. 46 f.

ity in a variety of ways in order to produce as nearly as possible a series of five-stress lines. Obviously it would be a possible alternative to follow the line division of the original editions, and the question is whether any useful purpose would be served by doing so. I think perhaps it would. I am not sure that either McKerrow or Dr. Greg has said the last word on the subject. Mc-Kerrow, in fact, really says nothing specifically about it; the point would seem to be covered by his general statement that "I have as a rule, when a slight redivis-ion of the lines would result in adequate verse, so divided them." [4] Dr. Greg concludes that "as a rule no great importance attaches to the line division in early printed texts, and an editor may be mainly guided by his own sense of the fitness of the verse." [5] But if no great importance attaches to the line division in early printed texts, it may just as well be said that none attaches to that of modern editions, and that, in edi-tions intended for the informed student, the former will serve as well as the latter. That the line division cannot usually be recognized by the ear except in heavily end-stopped verse anybody can prove to him-self by listening to the speaking of the lines. If they can be read expressively without being redivided into normal lengths, there is no need at all to re-divide them. I remember what happened some years ago when, for the first time, I read *Macbeth* with a class of graduate students from the Folio text. This play is notoriously full of mislineation. I therefore noted conscientiously all the rearrangements of the editors for the purpose of pointing out the mislined passages to the students. But when we read the play, I gave up about the middle of the second scene. For the most part, the play read perfectly well as printed in the Folio and the assiduous tinkering of the editors seemed mere pedantry. When we remember that mislineation is more common in the later plays, we may wonder whether it does not go along with the greater freedom of Shakespeare's mature style, whether indeed "mis-lineation" is not in part Shakespeare's work. If it is, or even if there is a chance that it is, some editions should certainly preserve it.

It is evident, I hope, that, without considering the dialogue of the plays at all, there are a number of significant ways in which the practice of editors might depart from that to which we are accustomed. There is room for editions of Shakespeare different from those we have, editions which will serve some purposes better than they do. We need McKerrow's edition; perhaps we need several editions more or less like it. Indeed I think there is room for an edition which would reproduce the most authoritative text of each play with no editing at all except to correct undoubted mistakes and make good undoubted omissions. This would serve chiefly as a convenient substitute for fac-similes. Just so it would be welcome, since there is no complete set of reliable facsimiles of the Quartos and all facsimiles are expensive. I have made some experiments with a text of this kind which make me think the idea is practicable.

There is another kind of edition which I think might prove serviceable, one which would go into details of the performance of the plays on the stage. I am not prepared to say just how this would be done; I am prompted to suggest it by the profit I have gained from reading acting versions and by the way acting versions open the eyes of students. Acting versions of course adapt the play to the modern stage, whereas I should prefer an adaptation to the Elizabethan stage; besides they tend to be bewilderingly elaborate and sometimes arbitrary. But a stage version prepared with Shakespeare's stage in mind rather than ours and for the reader rather than the actor might prove a very interesting experiment.

I come now to my second proposition—that it is not inconceivable that in the future we can make better texts of Shakespeare than we have today. I do not foresee any drastic or sensational changes. As long as the current consensus of opinion about the authority of the texts is substantially correct, as I believe it is, there is no possibility of a drastic shake-up; that would follow only the upsetting of our notions of authority. I mean only that here and there we may be able to make small and unexciting changes with reasonable assurance that they bring us closer to Shakespeare's intentions. I believe that further study will at least give editors greater confidence in what they are doing and sometimes it may lead to real improvements in our texts. I shall consider just one example—the text of the First Folio.

The rehabilitation of the Quartos during the last

thirty years or more has perhaps put the Folio into the shade, but as it is still the sole source of our knowledge of half the plays it is highly important to understand it as well as we can. We can find out a good deal about it by observing the way in which it handled the texts which it reprinted from earlier Quartos. If we find that these, or many of them, were treated in the same way, we may suspect that the plays printed for the first time were also treated the same way so far as this treatment could be applied to a manuscript as well as to printed copy. Thus we may gain a clearer idea of the manuscripts that underlie the Folio texts, of the probable divergences of the latter from the former, and of the authority of the latter. I had better illustrate what I have in mind at once.

The authorities from Malone to the present day agree that the folio text of *1 Henry IV* was printed from the Fifth Quarto (1613). But if we make a detailed comparison of these two texts it soon becomes evident that they diverge frequently and sometimes in important ways. They by no means correspond as closely as the First and the Second Quartos of the same play or as most pairs of texts of which one is derived immediately from the other.

The differences between Q_5 and the Folio are found everywhere—in the stage directions, the speech prefixes, the punctuation, and the wording of the dialogue. I will give a few samples. The differences in the stage directions are not very numerous and many of them simply reword the Quarto direction more tersely or smoothly. But the Folio specifies a few entrances and exits not noted in the Quarto and makes one quite remarkable change at the beginning of I.ii.[6] There is really only one change in the speech prefixes, but it is very important: three speeches in II.iv which the Quarto gives to *Ross[ill]* are transferred to *Gad[s-hill]* and one which the Quarto gives to *Gad[shill]* is transferred to the prince. I will not attempt to explain the changes in punctuation except to say that there are some which signify how the lines are to be spoken where the Quarto fails to do so.

Of the changes in the dialogue, the most numerous perhaps are excisions of profanity, for which we all understand the motive and upon which I will not dwell. There are also, however, quite a few which convert limping lines into normal ones by adding a syllable or two. For example, "But this our purpose is twelue month old" (Q₅ I.i.28) becomes "But this our purpose is a tweluemonth old"; "In my faint slumbers, I by thee watcht" (II.iii.50) becomes "In my faint-slumbers, I by thee haue watcht"; "Whose temper I intend to staine" (V.ii.94) becomes "Whose worthy temper I intend to staine"; "I was not borne to yeeld, thou proud *Sot*" (V.iii.11) becomes "I was not borne to yeeld, thou haughty Scot." A number of elisions are marked which have the effect of making the rhythm more regular: "He questioned me: among the rest demanded" (Q₅ I.iii.47) becomes "He question'd me: Among the rest, demanded"; "What er'e *Harry Percie* then had said" (I.iii.71) becomes "What

---

[6] Q₅ *Enter Prince of Wales and Sir Iohn Falstaffe.* F *Enter Henry Prince of Wales, Sir Iohn Falstaffe, and Pointz.*

euer *Harry Percie* then had said"; "Then let not him
be slandered with reuolt" (I.iii.112) becomes "Then
let him not be sland'red with Reuolt"; "Proclaymed at
Market crosses, read in Churches" (V.i.73) becomes
"Proclaim'd at Market Crosses, read in Churches." A
number of changes seem designed to improve the
clarity and consonance of the text. For example, where
Q₅ reads (I.iii.25 ff.)

> Were as he sayes, not with such strength denied,
> As he delieuered to your Maiesty.
> Either enuie therefore, or misprision
> Is guiltie of this fault, and not my sonne.

the Folio substitutes

> Were (as he sayes) not with such strength denied
> As was deliuered to your Maiesty:
> Who either through enuy, or misprision
> Was guilty of this fault; and not my Sonne.

Where Q₅ reads "they take it already vpon their salua-
tion, that though I be but *Prince of Wales,* yet I am
King of *Curtesie;* and tell mee flatly, I am not proud
Iack, like *Falstalffe"* (II.iv.9 ff.), the Folio has "They
take it already vpon their confidence, that though I be
but Prince of Wales, yet I am the King of Curtesie:
telling me flatly I am no proud Iack like *Falstaffe."*
Elsewhere "This bald vnioynted chat of his (my Lord)
I answered indirectly (as I sayd)" (Q₅ I.iii.66) becomes
"Made me to answer indirectly (as I said.)"; "Neuer
did bare and rotten policy" (I.iii.108) becomes "Neuer
did base and rotten Policy"; "Albeit I make a hazard
of my head" (I.iii.128) becomes "Although it be with
hazard of my head"; "Yea on his part, Ile empty all

these veines" (I.iii.133) becomes "In his behalfe, Ile empty all these Veines"; "thou shalt haue a share in our purchase" (II.i.88) becomes "Thou shalt haue a share in our purpose"; "our plot is a good plot as euer was laid" (II.iii.17) becomes "our plot is as good a plot as euer was laid"; "Ile shew thee a present" (II.iv.30 f.) becomes "Ile shew thee a President"; "Death hath not strooke so faire a Deere to day" (V.iv.107) becomes "Death hath not strucke so fat a Deere to day." Where Q₅ makes Worcester say "Good Coosen giue me audience for a while" (I.iii.211), the Folio adds, as if this were not explicit enough, "And list to me." Some of these changes restore readings of Q₁ which had been corrupted in successive reprintings, but that Q₁ was not regularly collated is proved by passages in which the corruption is repaired by different means. For example, where the Folio makes the king say "But this our purpose is a tweluemonth old" (I.i.28) instead of "But this our purpose is twelue month old," Q₁ reads "But this our purpose now is twelue month old"; obviously it was not consulted.

Changes like these cannot be the result of chance or accident; they are deliberate. But who made them? All things considered, I think it is more likely than not that they were made at the time the Folio was printed. In other words, they are editorial; they were made to prepare the text of the play for readers. The only alternative is to suppose that they were made in the theater and this seems to me much less credible. The changes which repair the errors of earlier Quartos are not in the least likely to have been made in the theater, for presumably the actors for many years had acted the play from a prompt-book derived from the manuscript on which Q₁ is based. The other changes, or at least most of them, are such as I think would not commend themselves to the actors, would not seem to them worth while. It looks then, as if the Folio text was edited for printing in somewhat the same manner as the later Folios and the eighteenth-century texts were edited. The job was neither thoroughly nor altogether competently done, but it had, in a general way, the same purpose as the operations of any editor, to make good the obvious defects of the text and to put it in as intelligible form as possible for the reader.

Furthermore, if *1 Henry IV* was edited in this way, there is no reason to think that it would have been treated differently from other plays. The First Quarto was a perfectly good text, and while the Fifth had accumulated a number of typographical errors and other changes, it was still passable. If *1 Henry IV,* then, was given a bit of polish for its appearance in the First Folio, the same attention may just as well have been given other plays too. In fact, I suspect that it was. I am not prepared to report on other plays in the collection derived from printed copies with details such as I have given for *1 Henry IV,* but I believe that some of them at least will be found to show signs of the same kind of treatment. If so, we should be able to work out a sort of method which was followed in preparing these plays for publication, a set of editorial standards, as it were. This is of little consequence so far as the plays which may be studied in this way are concerned, for of course

we regard the earliest Quarto of each one as the authoritative text and pay little attention to reprints of
it. But suppose we examine the plays which appear for
the first time in the Folio and we find evidence there
of the treatment of the text by the same method. This
evidence will be harder to find, but it may be discover-
able just the same. At any rate, if we can detect the
editorial hand in the Folio texts which had not been
printed before, then we may have something. We may
be able to discount the editor's intervention and infer,
perhaps with assurance, some readings of the unedited
text. At least, we shall have a clearer idea of what we
are dealing with; we shall be better able to assess the
authority of the Folio texts.

I hope I have not given the impression that the idea
of the editing of the First Folio is new. On the contrary, it has often been speculated on, but no real consensus of opinion has been attained. As late as 1909
Pollard spoke of "the high probability that there was
no editorial meddling with the text of the plays [in the
Folio], as contrasted with such matters of form as their
division into acts and scenes and the supply of additional stage directions." [7] Thirty years later Dr. Greg
draws a quite different picture of the editing of the
Folio in which he says that the plays "underwent a
good deal of modernization, and general tidying up in
spelling, punctuation, grammar, metre, and so on." [8]

---

[7] *Shakespeare Folios and Quartos* (London, Methuen and Company, 1909), p. 129. But in 1917 Pollard wrote (*Shakespeare's Fight with the Pirates,* London, A. Moring, Ltd., 1917, p. 98): "the First Folio must be regarded as an *edited* text." He added, "How far the editing ex-tended is a question of detail."   [8] *Op. cit.,* p. 155.

This is exactly what I have been illustrating. But what has never been done is to go beyond general statements or illustrations drawn from a single play and to define the editorial work done on the Folio on a broad scale. A comprehensive assay of this work may sharpen our understanding of the text of 1623, may enable us to edit it with greater confidence, and may even show us how to improve it.[9]

9 Perhaps an example will show the kind of improvement (i.e. recovery of what Shakespeare actually wrote from what was printed) I have in mind. It must be widely known that F often substitutes *heaven* for *God* in plays printed from earlier Quarto texts. We are therefore entitled to suspect that the same substitution was sometimes made in texts printed in F for the first time. In fact, it has already been suspected in a few places. At *John* V.vii.60, where F reads "Where heauen he knowes how we shall answer him," Sidney Walker (*A Critical Examination of the Text of Shakespeare*, 1860, i. 215) has proposed reading "God he knows" and at least two editors have followed him. Walker has also suggested the same substitution in *The Two Gentlemen* IV. iv. 112, "As (heauen it knowes) I would not haue him speed." Of *Measure for Measure* II. iv. 2 ff. ("heauen hath my empty words, Whilst my Inuention, hearing not my Tongue, Anchors on *Isabell:* heauen in my mouth, As if I did but onely chew his name") Dover Wilson remarks that " 'his name' (l. 5) makes it possible that Shakespeare wrote 'God' here and that the F. 'heaven' was substituted in accordance with the blasphemy law." It is also a fact that the relative frequency of *God* and *heaven* (which of course cannot be expected to be constant) differs greatly in different plays. *God* (meaning the Christian deity) occurs not at all in *The Two Gentlemen* and *Measure,* twice in *The Merry Wives,* 9 times each in *Errors* and *John,* 12 times in *Twelfth Night,* 14 in *Macbeth,* 15 in *All's Well,* 16 in *The Taming of the Shrew,* 18 in *As You Like It,* 23 in *1 Henry VI,* 31 in *3 Henry VI,* 54 in *2 Henry VI,* 61 in *Henry V. Heaven* occurs 4 times in *The Taming of the Shrew,* 7 in *Errors,* 9 in *Henry V,* 10 each in *The Two Gentlemen* and *As You Like It,* 16 in *1 Henry VI,* 18 in *Macbeth,* 19 in *2 Henry VI,* 21 in *3 Henry VI,* 23 in *All's Well,* 25 in *The Merry Wives,* 42 in *Measure,* 47 in *John.* (In a few plays which are thought to have been printed from Shakespeare's MSS the figures are as follows: *Dream,* God 8, heaven 6; *Merchant,* God 16, heaven 17; *Love's Labour's Lost,* God 26, heaven 19; *Much Ado,* God 54, heaven 1; *Richard*

The text of Shakespeare is not a close-cropped field from which no more can be gleaned. Though it does not seem likely that it will be drastically reconsidered in the future, it still repays intensive study intelligently directed.

II, God 57, heaven 29.) These figures suggest that, in *Measure*, *The Merry Wives*, and *John*, Shakespeare's *God* is most likely to have been diluted to *heaven*. One would first suspect *heaven* in the speech of certain characters and in stock phrases where *God* is common, such as "God save," "God help," "God shield," "to serve God." E.g., it is odd, in view of her record in other plays, that Mrs. Quickly in *The Merry Wives* uses *heaven* 6 times and *God* not once, and when she says "Sure, one of you do's not serue heauen well, that you are so cross'd" (IV.v. 130) it seems quite legitimate to suspect that Shakespeare wrote "serve God." When it is remembered that, in plays printed in quarto from Shakespeare's MSS, *heaven* is more often dissyllabic than monosyllabic (except in *by heaven*), the meter may serve as guide to some substitutions of this kind.—Professor Price provides me with another example. He notes that *bear-ward* (or *bear-herd*) occurs in *Much Ado* II.i. 43 as *Berrord* and in *2 Henry IV* I.ii.192 as *Berod*. (It also occurs in *2 Henry VI* V.i.149, 210 as *Berard* and *Bearard*.) Therefore there is every likelihood that *Beare-heard*, coming from the mouth of Christopher Sly (*Shrew* Ind.ii.21), is an editorial sophistication.

Problems in the Editing of Shakespeare: Interpretation

By MATTHEW W. BLACK

THE INTERPRETATION of lines and passages of Shake-speare in the last two decades has fallen somewhat behind other lines of endeavor. Many qualified students, perceiving that the great nineteenth-century editors had carried explication as far as their knowledge would permit, have turned to such larger problems as the ideology, imagery, and symbolism of his plays as a whole. Others have set about the unearthing of new facts, with such success, quantitatively at least, that it is doubtful whether any one mind, in the working hours of an ordinary lifetime, will ever again be able to assimilate all that is known about Shakespeare, so as to undertake a fully authoritative interpretation of the canon as a whole.

At all events, the present writer, far from entertaining so ambitious a hope, has begun to despair of living long enough to find out all that is to be known about a single play, *King Richard II*. And only the sternest selection within that limit can be presented here. If, therefore, this paper may be permitted to adopt the eminently practical custom of Elizabethan booksellers whereby an abridged table of contents was displayed as a subtitle, its subtitle will be something like this: "A brief indication of the various kinds of work which—in my opinion—will make for future progress in the interpretation of debated lines and passages in Shakespeare, with illustrations drawn from the play of *King Richard II*, exclusive of passages in which there is uncertainty about the text." In other words, the nature of a few representative problems is made clear as a necessary prelude to a new attempt at their solution; but the paper is organized around the method of solution.

If my readers learn anything new, it will be from the illustrations and not from the methods and devices employed. The interpreter has not been presented with the intellectual equivalent of those chemical analyses, revelations by infra-red rays, and comparison projectors which gladden the hearts and speed the labors of those whose province is the text. He is dependent, as heretofore, solely upon the accumulation of new facts, the intelligent and imaginative application of the facts he has, and the habit of brooding over an obscure passage until it yields a meaning.

I do believe, however, that a word may still be said on the question, which meaning? For the interpreters of Shakespeare, from his Restoration adapters to the author of the latest note in the scholarly journals, have as a body been myriad-minded in the worst sense of the word: they have never, as a body, agreed on which meaning they should seek; and I think it could be demonstrated that not one of those who have been large-minded enough to set up a principle has succeeded in adhering to it in every instance. We have had interpreters whose ideal meaning was that which would be most pleasing aesthetically to a poetic reader of the text; others who sought the meaning most effective in the theatre; still others whose object was to recreate from the text a Shakespeare who should conform to their conception of him as an omniscient intellect, an infallible intelligence, a flawless artist, or a profound moralist; still others whose judgment was swayed by some preconceived theory as to the authorship of the plays; others who sought merely to make the plays intelligible to a schoolboy, or even to make some rival editor look like a fool. Above all, we have had editors whose conclusions were based, here on one of these principles, there on another.

Yet ever and anon the best of them, at their best, have struck out a comment or a paraphrase so manifestly, convincingly right that we say instinctively, "That is what Shakespeare meant." And I take this to be the best possible answer to our question: the meaning we want is the meaning Shakespeare intended.

Unfortunately, of course, this is no real answer, but only a restatement of the question. What sort of man, and what sort of writer was Shakespeare? are questions infinitely harder than what he meant in a given passage. To some extent, moreover, they beg the question, since what he meant in the passage enters into our conception of him as man and artist. Fortunately, however, the great majority of his lines are of such clarity that not even his editors have been able to raise a doubt as to what they mean; we have only to reflect the prevailing light into the lesser darkness.

I suggest, therefore, that this restatement of the question of what we are looking for is neither obvious nor futile. It has the negative advantage of ruling out those interpreters whose judgment is swayed by too narrow a theory, or whose approach is too exclusively that of the study or that of the stage. On the positive side, it gives focus and vitality to the endless investigation which editing entails. In literal truth one takes all knowledge for one's province. In my own experience thus far, I have yet to encounter a completely irrelevant fact, or a comment so foolish as to be utterly without value. But of course one works hardest at the most promising lodes: one reads and rereads the other plays, attempting to develop a sort of sixth sense for the individual accent of Shakespeare within the idiom of his age; meanwhile one casts as wide a net as possible into Elizabethan literature and history, reconstructing, as well as one's limitations will permit, Shakespeare's world; in particular I have come to believe that the comparison of the plays with their sources is a field that still contains a richer harvest than it has so far yielded.

In other words, we shall progress by means of editors who have the time and energy to glean new crops in fields which have the deceptive air of being worked out. I only add that inquiries so disparate—and to them is added the whole distracting and fascinating business of the text—inquiries so disparate need a focus, and their natural focus is the man writing. That is the figure which should preside in the mind of the editor when he sets down his commentary.

Interpretation of Shakespeare's writing should square in every respect with a humanly believable concept of Shakespeare the man—an Elizabethan poet-dramatist writing, a little hurriedly, on paper, with a quill pen. I emphasize the phrase "humanly believable." His mind, however justly we praise its capacity and its superb balance, must never be magnified to embrace the combined erudition of all his critics. His artistic genius must not be degraded into a sort of superhuman ingenuity which deliberately planned the innumerable subtleties which aesthetic critics have detected. Without impugning his universality, we must picture him as a man of his time. Without detracting from his greatness we must remind ourselves continually that this was a man, and keep our controlling image of him humanly believable.

If I speak with some feeling on this editorial principle, it is because it is crucial; because the best of Shakespeare's editors have fallen short of it to a degree and with a frequency that proclaims it almost impossible to achieve; and particularly because I attribute to it certain flecks of light—satisfying to me, at least—which I hope I have been able to throw on the meaning of the obscurities in *Richard II*.

By emphasizing the man behind the plays, a valuable emphasis is thrown upon the problem of chronology. Since the plays themselves are our principal witnesses as to what he was and how his mind and art developed, no pains can be spared in determining dates and sequence, not for the barren satisfaction of solving a puzzle, but because the man writing in 1596 was not quite the same as in 1593. And since Shakespeare the dramatist was demonstrably of a conservative turn, one who clung to what had proved its worth, who gave his experiments a thorough testing before he passed on, an editor must not only work out a complete chronology by which he is ready to stand or fall, but he must also know by heart not only the play he is working on, but those which precede and follow it.

In this regard the play of *Richard II* is especially interesting. The total impression it gives is that Shakespeare enjoyed writing it. This is, to be sure, not provable; but it has some value as an impression shared by editors who differ from one another in temperament and views. If he did enjoy it, it was most probably because in *Richard II,* by a fortunate choice of subject, he was able for the first time to make the poet he wanted to be, the happy servant of the dramatist he needed to be. This newly achieved duality of poet and playwright makes him a different artist from the skilled apprentice of *Richard III* as well as from the past master of the mature plays. He was for the time delightedly experimenting with the dramatic value of the arts and devices of rhetoric, word-play, and poetry. And this brings me to my first illustration.

In III.ii.147-173, King Richard has returned from Ireland to be staggered by three pieces of terrible news: from the first, the news that the usurper Bolingbroke has landed, he recovers by thinking of his divine right as king; from the second, Salisbury's report of the disbanding of Richard's Welsh supporters, he again rallies, but less buoyantly; the third, Scroope's tidings that his favorites have been executed, leads him to taste the voluptuousness of despair in a famous meditation on the death of kings.

> Within the hollow Crowne
> That rounds the mortall Temples of a King,
> Keepes Death his Court, and there the Antique sits
> Scoffing his State, and grinning at his Pompe,
> Allowing him a breath, a little Scene,
> To Monarchize, be fear'd, and kill with lookes,
> Infusing him with selfe and vaine conceit,
> As if this Flesh, which walles about our Life,
> Were Brasse impregnable: and humor'd thus,
> Comes at the last, and with a little Pinne
> Bores through his Castle Walls, and farwell King.

Humor'd thus: who is humored and in what sense? We turn to the *NED*. It gives "indulged" for the participle of the verb, but also "humoured" as an adjective, obsolete except in compounds, but good Elizabethan meaning "in a (specified) humour." At least three meanings are therefore possible: (1) Death having thus indulged himself; (2) the king having thus been indulged; (3) while the king is in this humor. Hopefully we turn to the editors and other authorities, to find of course that they are divided. Schmidt in his *Lexicon* and the Clarendon editors accept either (1) or (3). Abbott in his *Grammar* chooses (2), as do Watt and Newbolt. Rann and Lobban favor (1); and if theirs be judged no very impressive suffrages, they are strongly supported by Dover Wilson, quoting *Merchant of Venice* IV.iii.40–43:

> You'll ask me, why I rather choose to have
> A weight of carrion flesh than to receive

> Three thousand ducats: I'll not answer that:
> But say it is my humor.

Herford wavers between (2) and (3). Verity says the sense is clear, but does not say which sense. The rest of the editors either say nothing or follow one of those quoted. If we simply count the votes, the first reading, with three clear and two doubtful adherents, would prevail. But to complete the present editor's dilemma, he finds the third, the comparatively unsupported one, infinitely the best—on purely poetic grounds. The suggestion in the line

> Infusing him with selfe and vaine conceit,

that while the king is in this vainglorious humor Death takes a special, grimmer pleasure in destroying him, is so ironical that I cannot but prefer it. "Those whom the gods would destroy"—and Death is a god.

Here then is a typical problem. What shall I print? Here are several meanings, all justifiable from the context, all possible to the flexible syntax of the day, all supported by competent authorities. No very definite considerations of stage effectiveness are involved. To set my own judgment of poetry against that of Clark and Wright, Sir Henry Newbolt, and Dr. Wilson, is a duty from which the air of presumptuousness can be a little cleared by hiding it in brackets. There remains the man writing in the closing months of 1595. Can we get anything more from him? Fortunately, I think we can. For this so-called ambiguity is not unique. Others exactly like it occur all through the plays, but they are especially numerous in *Richard II,* in *John* just before it, and in the two parts of *Henry IV* which followed. If the "ambiguity" were unique, it might be an accident due to haste, and we would be entitled to take it as we prefer. But a humanly believable Shakespeare can hardly have been unaware that he had written passages like this again and again. What would he reply if we could ask him what he meant? Would he say, like Browning, that he had forgotten, and commend us to divine guidance? A working dramatist is more conscious of his intentions. Would he express surprise at the multiple meanings? Not the lover of words, alert as few have been to their many-sidedness. Would he, then, drop the accolade on Herford, or Newbolt, or Wilson, and say, "This great man, and he alone, has understood me"? It is possible, of course. But is there not a likelier answer, from a writer famous for word-play in an age of word-play? Might he not simply say, "I meant all these things"?

I am not suggesting that "humor'd thus" came where it is with the deliberateness of a pun, but rather that in the heat of composing these passionate lines Shakespeare hit upon a word and a construction that suggest all the kinds of *humoring* in his imaginary situation, a phrase that strikes, not a single tone, but a chord of three notes; and that minded as he was, he cannot have been unaware of it. A musician might remark that in a chord one note carries the melody and the others accompany and enrich it. So much the better for our metaphor, so long as all the notes are heard together.

But enough—if not too much—as to the editorial imagination. Let me hasten to add that the interpreter of Shakespeare needs facts most of all, especially facts about Elizabethan English and about Shakespeare's use of his sources. In the first act of *Richard II* he twice (I.i.92,iii.286) uses the locution "Looke what." Editors have either maintained a discreet silence, presumably taking "Look" in our colloquial sense, since they set it off by a comma; or they assume some archaic meaning for "Look," such as "Look for," [1] with "what" as direct object. But Professor Eccles [2] shows beyond doubt that "Look what" is an Elizabethan idiom for "Whatever," a reading which makes the best possible sense of both lines. In III.i.24, Bolingbroke complains that because of Bushy and Greene he has sigh'd his "English breath in forraine Clouds." The commentators find several possible explanations: it may mean no more than that Bolingbroke has been forced to live abroad; there may be a pun on clouds of breath and clouds of heaven; it may be a piece of fancy, a bold conceit, repeating *Romeo and Juliet* I.i.139-40:

> With tears augmenting the fresh morning's dew,
> Adding to clouds more clouds with his deep sighs.

But Wilson in his edition of the play (1939, p. 181) suspects that it is "probably a piece of Elizabethan science, rather than a bold conceit"; and I understand from Professor John Arthos that, in a forthcoming study of poetic diction and its sources, he is inclined to favor Wilson's conjecture.

[1] Cf. *The Tragedy of Richard the Second,* ed. Hardin Craig (1912), p. 151.   [2] *JEGP* XLII (1943), 386–400.

The word *infection* in Gaunt's famous lines on England (II.i.46–47):

> This Fortresse built by Nature for her selfe,
> Against infection, and the hand of warre:

has given rise to a great deal of comment. It could mean pestilence; it could be a misprint for *infestion,* that is, infestation or invasion, and so on. The similarity of the thought to that in Daniel's *Civil Wars* (Book IV, stanza 90):

> Neptune keepe out from thy imbraced Ile
> This foul contagion of iniquitie.

was noted by the Clarendon editors in 1869; but by comparing the whole passage with the whole of Daniel's Book IV, Reyher and Wilson have shown that Shakespeare was indebted to Daniel's ideas throughout, and therefore almost certainly in this instance. Whereupon the meaning becomes fully clear: no emendation is necessary; *infection* here as in Daniel means "moral contamination; . . . communication of harmful opinions or beliefs" (*NED*); "bloody-mindedness and civil strife" (Wilson).

As to the need of further work on Shakespeare's reading, not only comparing his text with known sources but also casting a wider net in search of new sources, I offer two further examples. In V.i.3–4 the Queen exclaims:

> This way the King will come: this is the way
> To *Iulius Caesars* ill-erected Tower.

No editor of *Richard II* or of *Richard III,* where Buckingham is made to inform Prince Edward that this medieval tradition is "upon record" (III.i.74), has told us where Shakespeare found in print the notion that Caesar built the Tower of London. It was undoubtedly a matter of oral tradition; Stow in his *Survay of London* (1598) says "it hath beene the common opinion." But he adds that "some have written it," though (contemptuously) "of none assured ground," and the reference in *Richard III* clearly implies a printed source. In his *Topographical Dictionary* (1925, p. 520), Sugden lists two plays, *Edward I* and the original text of *Sir Thomas More,* and a novel, Deloney's *Thomas of Reading,* in which the dramatist might have seen a reference previous to the writing of *Richard III*; but one doubts that Shakespeare would have thought of a statement in a work of fiction as "upon record," and doubts still more that the plays and novel were what Stow was alluding to: he almost certainly had a chronicler or chroniclers in mind. But the legend is not in Holinshed or Hall, nor in Geoffrey or any of the published medieval chronicles. An article by G. L. Frost [3] documents the matter for the first time, and reveals that—so far as is known at present—the notion was first placed "upon record" by the chronicler Nicholas Trivet (1258?–1328?) in "Les Cronicles qe frere N. Trevet escript a dame Marie la fille mon seigneur le roi d'Engleterre le filtz Henri" (B.M. MS Arundel 56). A recent article by H. Nearing [4] adds many *loci,* among them several, such as the *Scala-*

[3] "Caesar and Virgil's Magic in England," *MLN,* LI (1936), 431–33.
[4] "Julius Caesar and the Tower of London," *MLN,* LXIII (1948), 228–33.

chronica of Sir Thomas Gray (d. 1369?) and *The Parlement of the Thre Ages,* a dream-poem of the fourteenth-century alliterative revival, which suggest that, as might be expected, the legend became popular chiefly through poets and the less serious historians. Trivet's statement was brought within Shakespeare's ken through Lydgate's *Serpent of Division,* a prose life of Caesar written in 1422, but republished in 1559 and quoted by Grafton (whom Stow disliked!) in his *Chronicle at Large* (1569), a likely place for Shakespeare to see it. He could also have found it in a second reprinting of Lydgate, with *Gorboduc,* in 1590. Nearing's work thus suggests a new title, Lydgate's *Serpent of Division,* to be scanned for Shakespearean parallels, and another, Grafton's *Chronicle at Large,* which the dramatist has long been thought to have known, but which has manifestly not been sifted as carefully as it needs to be. And inspection of the probable printed sources, even in advance of a complete comparison, gives us something a little firmer than mere conjecture for the interpretation of the obscure word *ill-erected* in the speech of Richard II's queen. For the passage in Lydgate, and Grafton's citation of it, emphasize that Caesar's purpose in erecting the Tower was to commemorate his name and his victory over the British King Cassibelan. Hence such glosses as "erected for bad purposes," "inauspiciously erected," "erected with evil results" probably miss the mark. It is more likely that the Queen connects the Tower with the rise of an earlier usurper than Henry IV and the downfall of an earlier English king than

Richard. It was erected to commemorate an ill day for England, similar for her to that which Richard is living through.

In like fashion it is to be hoped that further search of the religious literature of his age may show that Shakespeare could have heard or read the explanation of "the needle's eye" as the Arab name for a narrow gate in a city wall. It is not in the index to the Parker Society, nor in any commentary on Shakespeare I have been able to find. Modern students of the Scriptures seem not to have located the idea in print before the middle of the nineteenth century, when it was put forward as new by Lord Nugent in *Lands Classical and Sacred* (1846, I,326). All that Nugent actually says is that the arch for foot traffic in a particular town, Hebron, was called "the needle's eye," and that if all similar gates were so called in Biblical times, we have an easy and comforting solution to the simile of the rich man and the camel. A writer in *The Expository Times* (IX, 1897-98, pp. 387-89), presumably James Hastings, the editor, remarks that "Lord Nugent's evidence for the name of the gate is not very strong, and . . . never seems to have been strengthened"; while Post, in the article on "Camel" in the *Dictionary of the Bible* (1898) declares that "the needle's eye" as applied to a gate is a fabrication. An irrelevant but distracting element in the puzzle is the argument over the meaning of "camel," whether it means the beast, or a "cable rope," as suggested in the margin of the Geneva Bible. But as Noble points out in *Shakespeare's Biblical*

Knowledge (1935, pp. 95–96), when Shakespeare was
writing *Richard II* V.iv.17–18:

> It is as hard to come, as for a Camell
> To thred the posterne of a Needle's eye.

he had not recently been perusing the narrative in the
ordinary Genevan, since his metaphor of *posterne*
shows that he is thinking of the beast and not of the
cable. According to Ginsburg (*Athenaeum*, April 28,
1883, p. 542), this is the Hebrew intention: "Without
being acquainted with the language of the Talmud,
Shakespeare clearly saw that the passage in *Matthew*
XIX.24 was a proverbial saying in which the largest
animal and the smallest aperture were selected to express an impossibility. Hence, with the true genius of
a great poet, he not only correctly, but most beauti-
fully and poetically renders it." But whence the
posterne? Unless some source can be discovered for
this association of images, we are left with coincidence
as the only explanation—a happy coincidence, far
from unparalleled elsewhere in Shakespeare's writing,
but a very remarkable one: Shakespeare, who repeats
the image of needle-threading in a play close to *Richard II* in date (*King John* V.iv.11: "unthread the rude
eye of rebellion") without any such complication, is
here mysteriously and without external suggestion
moved to adorn the needle's eye with precisely the metaphor which Lord Nugent, two and a half centuries
later, discovered, or pretended to discover, in the parlance of an obscure Arab town, a metaphor which has
so much appeal for anxious sinners, especially rich

ones, that it has become widely known! It is almost easier to believe that Lord Nugent had been reading *King Richard II*.

But facts by themselves are seldom enough, and in the interpretation of one highly figurative passage in *Richard II* the accumulation of nine typed pages of facts tells little more than is explained, though of course only in general terms, by the passage itself, and completely fails to save the interpreter from the necessity of protracted brooding. I refer to the speech of Sir John Bushy when attempting to comfort the Queen who, despite her promise made at the parting, is grieving—prophetically enough—over Richard's absence (II.ii.16–29):

> *Bush.* Each substance of a greefe hath twenty shadows
> Which shewes like greefe it selfe, but is not so:
> For sorrowes eye, glazed with blinding teares,
> Diuides one thing intire, to many obiects,
> Like perspectiues, which rightly gaz'd vpon
> Shew nothing but confusion, ey'd awry,
> Distinguish forme: so your sweet Maiestie
> Looking awry vpon your Lords departure,
> Finde shapes of greefe, more than himselfe to waile,
> Which look'd on as it is, is naught bu[t] shadowes
> Of what it is not: then thrice-gracious Queene,
> More then your Lords departure weep not,
>   more's not seene;
> Or if it be, 'tis with false sorrowes eie,
> Which for things true, weepe thing imaginary.

It will be seen that, as often, the imagery is not the only difficulty in the speech. For some reason which the historical grammars do not adequately explain, the singular verb *shewes* in the second line (reinforced by *is*, so that it cannot be dismissed as the mere addition of an *s* by the printer) stands where we should expect the plural. A new and more searching investigation of the Elizabethan mind in its dealing with collective nouns would be needed if the sense of the whole depended—fortunately it does not—on knowing precisely what single entity in the picture "shows like grief itself but is not so." The word *Like* in the fifth line may be taken three ways: (1) the *obiects* are like perspectives; (2) looking at grief with its shadows is like looking at perspectives; (3) as correlative with *so* in the seventh line—and it can hardly combine all three of these, or the third and either of the others. The antecedent of *which* in the tenth line apears to be *departure* two lines above, but turns out otherwise. There is also a quibble, inverted to match the perspective, in *rightly* and *awry,* which first mean "at right angles" and "obliquely"; then, inversely, *awry* becomes "rightly for a perspective (that is, awry) but wrongly for grief." The literal phrase *as it is* completes this second antithesis and mercifully ends a minor involution.

But it is of course on the optics of the passage, and Shakespeare's knowledge of the optical toys and devices of his time that we need information. And the commentators supply it in their notes on *perspective.* We hear of pictures cut into strips, and the strips pasted on parallel indentations in a board in such fashion that when looking straight at the board one saw a confused piece of work, but by looking from just the proper angle on the left one saw a picture of Henry the Great of France, and similarly from the right, that of his Queen. We hear of skillful experiments with juxtaposed drawings in true and inverted perspective; of variants of the ridged pictures which showed a picture from the front and confusion from the side; of round crystal glasses, the convex surface cut into faces, the concave smooth; of "anamorphosis" glasses or "perspicils" which produced regular figures from distracted lines or a single portrait from a multitude of little faces; of the telescope; of a glass in which one man might see another man's image and not his own (presumably the distorting mirrors of the present-day amusement park); of Holbein's "The Ambassadors," in which a curious object in the foreground, resembling a heap of fish bones, is seen from the side to be a human skull; of Shakespeare's uses of the word *perspective* in other plays, which are inconclusive, except that nowhere among them does he use "perspective" for "telescope" as Beaumont and Fletcher do, so that that meaning here would be a doubtful one.

The number and variety of editorial explanations is sufficient evidence of the difficulty of the passage. Unfortunately, some of the devices mentioned, such as the anamorphoscope, are first described in the seventeenth century, and it is guesswork that they were known to Shakespeare in 1595. Among those of earlier date, however, are (1) the perspective glass, a mirror or lens which distorts, and (2) the picture which presents a different appearance from the front and from the side or sides. And these two devices not only form the

basis of the imagery, but are, as I have said, described
sufficiently for the purpose of interpretation in the
passage itself. Thus the sifting of the available facts
confirms the interpretation but does not really determine it. On the contrary, the irrelevant fact brought
out by the commentators that a distorting glass was
called a perspective (for Shakespeare in this passage
uses the word only for the changeable picture) has be-
mused critics into eying the whole matter awry. The
distorting-glass image, with which the passage begins,
breaks off after four lines; the changeable-picture
image, ambiguously connected to its predecessor by
Like, occupies the next five lines; the distorting-glass
then reappears in the five remaining lines, framing
but not quite dominating the whole.

In dealing with passages like this I take a careful
paraphrase to be the best editorial instrument. I have
accordingly devised the following (ll. 16 to the middle
of 26): Each substance of a grief has twenty delusive
semblances (*NED* <Shadow, 6. fig.>, the familiar
sense when in contrast with *substance*), an unreal appearance which, added to the substance, makes grief
seem greater than it is; for Sorrow's eye, glazed with
blinding tears, distorts and shatters the true appearance into many objects, to look at which is like looking at perspectives (or, just possibly, the objects themselves are like the parts of perspectives), which, gazed
upon from the front, show nothing but confusion;
eyed obliquely, present distinguishable form: so your
sweet majesty, looking obliquely upon your lord's
departure, as though it were a perspective—which you

ought not to do—distinguish forms of grief, shadows surrounding the substance, that is, his departed self; whereas if you could only see his departure as it is, you would see that these forms *are* naught but the shadows of shadows.

After dealing to the best of one's ability with a passage like this, it becomes a little difficult to reconstruct the mental processes of those editors who have erected their altars to Shakespeare as a flawless artist. Bushy's speech is hastily written, and it is difficult not to suppose that its author would have clarified it if he had ever gone over it critically. A number of editors do scold about it, and I doubt not Ben Jonson would have listed the four lines on *perspectives* among the thousand to be blotted. Yet by brooding over it long enough one sees that it is at any rate not the ordinary "mixed" metaphor; it is not a dominant figure interrupted by a subsidiary and irrelevant one. It is a combination of two similes from the field of optics, the second and more complex one introduced when the first proved inadequate. Its weakness is rhetorical, consisting in a let-down at the end, through a perfunctory and repetitive return to the original simile. The whole effect is confusing rather than really confused; and it is, after all, no part of the job of an editor of Shakespeare to object to "the majesty and riches of his mind."

The First Quarto of
Titus Andronicus

꽃

By HEREWARD T. PRICE

BEFORE WE CAN SPEAK with certainty about any one
dramatist we must carry out a large number of investigations into the usage of other dramatists. What
I have to say is in effect a report of work in progress. I
have not reached finality nor is anybody in our genera-
tion likely to get as far as that. Here I shall sketch out
results that appear to me to be fairly certain, but they
would be much more certain if Shakespeare's con-
temporaries had been studied as thoroughly as Shakespeare himself.

The First Quarto of *Titus Andronicus* is perhaps
the most famous and the most interesting of the Shakespearean Quartos. It is famous because, after scholars
had for generations presumed its existence, the unique
copy was at last discovered in Sweden. It is interesting
because of the many unique problems connected with
it. In some respects it is much nearer to Shakespeare
than any other version of the play. It alone gives the
lines (I.i, after l. 35):

> and at this day, [Titus hath]
> To the monument of that *Andronicy*
> Done sacrifice of expiation,
> And slaine the Noblest prisoner of the *Gothes*.

Titus had not performed these actions yet; he was to do them almost immediately in the course of the scene. The passage contains a glaring blunder, which Q₂ corrects by cutting it out, leaving a broken line to betray where the cut took place. For the purposes of this paper it is only interesting as lending support to the other evidence we possess that the copy for Q₁ was in Shakespeare's handwriting. The blunder is not likely to have survived long in a prompt-copy.

Q₂ was printed from a copy of Q₁, and here I quote Dr. J. Q. Adams:

It is obvious that the copy of the First Quarto supplied by White to the printer of the Second Quarto was seriously defective at the bottom of the last three leaves, K2, K3, and K4, rendering it impossible for the typesetter to read parts of the thirteen lines, and all of five lines, and deceiving him as to the conclusion of the play. As a result, trusting to conjecture, and when necessary resorting to improvisation, the compositor, or proof reader supplied in whole or in part twenty-three lines, of which fourteen are textually incorrect, and nine have no rightful place in the tragedy.[1]

Several interesting questions arise. We should like to know who supplied to the printer of Q₂ the correction of the blunder in Act I. It must have been somebody close either to Shakespeare or to the theater and it is therefore difficult to explain why the printer of Q₂ could not get a good text. Further we catch the print-

[1] Shakespeare's *Titus Andronicus,* The First Quarto 1594 Reproduced in facsimile from the unique copy in the Folger Shakespeare Library with an introduction by Joseph Quincy Adams (New York and London, Charles Scribner's Sons, 1936), p. 24. See also J. S. Y. Bolton in *PMLA,* XLIV (1929), 776–780, and R. B. McKerrow in *The Library,* 4th Ser., XV (1934), 49–53.

ing-house in the act of vamping out lines of fairly
normal blank verse. Q₁ ends:

> Her life was beastlie and deuoide of pittie,
> And being dead let birds on her take pittie.

The editor of Q₂ wrote a much more normal ending.
He ends:

> Her life was beastly and deuoid of pitty,
> And being so shall haue like want of pitty.
> See iustice done on Aron that dambd *Moore,*
> By whome our heauy haps had their beginning:
> Then afterwards to order well the state;
> That like euents may ne'er it ruinate.

The couplet at the end appears to make this version
more Shakespearean than Q₁. But in *Titus* we find that
Shakespeare avoids ending scenes or acts with a couplet. Act V ends in Q₁ like all the other acts except
Act II in lines that avoid the heavy thump of the couplet, and this uniformity of style provides us with still
more reason to believe that Q₁ is close to Shakespeare.

I wish to limit the discussion here to one particular
problem, namely, the spellings of Q₁. Many scholars
have already made valuable contributions to our
knowledge of Elizabethan spelling.[2]

In the first place it is necessary to formulate the
problem clearly. Our task is to decide whether the
spellings of Q₁ give us any reason to believe that it was

[2] See especially in respect to our problem J. Dover Wilson, "Spellings
and Misprints in the Second Quarto of *Hamlet*," in *Essays and Studies
by Members of the English Association,* X (1924), 36–60. See also the
same author's *The Manuscript of Shakespeare's Hamlet* (Cambridge
University Press, 1934), pp. 114–117.

printed from copy in Shakespeare's handwriting. Professor Dover Wilson has collected evidence which in his opinion proves that Shakespeare himself wrote the copy from which the compositor set up Q₂ of *Hamlet*. But neither Professor Dover Wilson nor anybody else has faced the problem of spelling in Elizabethan poetry. Now Elizabethan English was incredibly clipped, much more so than English is nowadays. The compositors, however, in setting up prose, ignored the clippings and chose for their normal spelling the full form of the word. Elizabethan poets, and especially the dramatists, were eager to have their lines properly read or spoken and so they took great pains to use spelling which should indicate the elisions or the shortenings they desired. As we shall see, Shakespeare was so thorough as to be almost pedantic in subordinating spelling to pronunciation.

The question is, then, whether we can find in Q₁ of *Titus* any method of spelling that constitutes such a pattern or "Gestalt" as to show an individual mind at work, and then whether this "individuality" resembles other texts, like Q₂ of Hamlet, which are supposed to be based on Shakespeare's handwriting, and finally, whether this individuality, or idosyncrasy, or pattern differs so markedly from the usage of other dramatists that we can say with some confidence about a particular text, "This is really based on Shakespeare's handwriting."

Unfortunately this paper is, as I have said, only a report of work in progress, and I have not been able to follow up all the clues that have suggested themselves.

For example, we ought to know what were the usages observed by Danter, the printer of Q$_1$. For this important study I have had no time, nor has it been possible for me to make a thorough study of spelling in other dramatists. I ignore misprints and punctuation in *Titus,* since they would make this paper far too long.

For purposes of comparison I have taken the following Quartos: *Hamlet* (1604); *Romeo and Juliet* (1599); *Love's Labour's Lost* (1598); 2 *Henry IV* (1600); *Midsummer Night's Dream* (1600); *Much Ado* (1600); *Merchant of Venice* (1600); and also the Quartos of *Venus and Adonis* and the *Rape of Lucrece,* which I consider separately.

In order to institute comparison with other authors I have taken Ben Jonson *Every Man out of his Humour,* 1600 Quarto, in the Malone Society Reprints, 1920 (1921), and Massinger *Beleeve as you List,* MS Egerton 2828, British Museum, in the Malone Society Reprints, 1927 (1928). I know quite well that a comparison with but two plays is not enough to establish a thesis. I am merely indicating the direction studies of this sort might take.

The whole world of Shakespearean scholarship owes an immense debt to Professor Dover Wilson for his pioneer work in bibliography. I am making his articles my point of departure and I wish to acknowledge unreservedly my obligations to him. On the other hand, as we all look at the same subjects with different interests, I shall arrange my data in different categories from those employed by Professor Dover

Wilson. This, of course, does not in any way lessen
either my debt to him or my appreciation of his
work.

I should like to consider the following categories of
Shakespearean spellings. There are first the metrical
spellings consisting of devices to show when sounds
should or should not be elided for purposes of meter.
Then there are the spellings one might be tempted to
call phonetic in that they are based on pronunciation.
These have nothing to do with meter. Then there is a
group of miscellaneous spellings which Shakespeare
preferred for no reason connected with pronunciation. And finally a list of certain single words which
Shakespeare habitually spells in a particular way so
that it appears to constitute an idiosyncrasy.

I

First, then, the metrical spellings. Elizabethan dramatists labored hard to make their spelling correspond
to the meter; that is to say, they were strict in indicating elisions, contractions, and the clipped syllable.
I do not know whether this minute care for accuracy
arose from the necessity of seeing that the actors did
not make a mess of the rhythm, but at any rate these
are the metrical spellings to which Shakespeare pays
special attention: contractions of –ed in the past tense
and the past participle; the contraction of –en; of
–est (the ending both of the second personal singular
and of the superlative); of –er (–or, –ur); of l in verbal
suffixes; of initial or final l, s, t, th in small words; and

finally the elision of a medial weak vowel in certain circumstances.

In order to show the pattern or idiosyncrasy of Shakespeare's spellings I shall take each class separately.

1. *–ed* of the weak verb. Shakespeare indicates the clipping of *–ed* after all consonants except *r* with almost meticulous pedantry. Thus, to take a few examples, we have *consumde, moude, lopt, promist, shipt.* A few characteristic forms are *grac'd* (II.i.27), *sad facde* (V.iii.67), *opt* (V.iii.108), *long tongude* (IV.ii.150), *pearst, skard* (IV.iv.31), *whitelimde* (IV.ii.98), *aduaunst* (IV.ii.157), *pronouncst* (III.i.50). He uses no apostrophes—*barred* is *bard*, *dimmed* is *dimd*. *Whitelimde* (that is, *whitelimed*) is mistaken for *whitelimbed* in Q₂, Q₃, and F₁. On the other hand, when the *–ed* is to be pronounced as a separate syllable, it is printed in full, as, for instance, in participles used as adjectives, as *beloued* (I.i.169, IV.ii.47), *armed* (IV.ii. 16) [but *armde* (I.i.136)]. Down to the present day this differentiation of spelling is important. Thus at the end of the line we have the feminine endings *conquered* (I.i.336), *abused* (II.iii.87), *murthered* (II.iii. 263), *discoueued* (II.iii.287), *mentioned* (V.i.107). Modern editors pick and choose here, printing *abus'd* and *mention'd* and leaving the others with *–ed* in full. I think they are probably wrong as to *abused* and *mentioned.*

Nobody can deny that Shakespeare went to a great deal of trouble in order to indicate the pronunciation he desired. In the case of *grac'd* and *facde* he probably thought that a phonetic spelling with *st* (*grast*, *fast*) would be ambiguous and suggest some connection with *grass* or *fast*. A spelling like *tradust* for *traduced* (*Hamlet* I.iv.18) cannot be misunderstood, but such a spelling was not possible for *grac'd* or *facde*.

Shakespeare usually writes *–ed* after *w,* and sometimes after *u,* as *moued* (II.iii.151), *sowed* (II.iv.39, 43), *ouerflowed and drownd* (III.i.230), *vnhallowed* (V.ii. 91, iii.14), but *showd* (II.iii.98). After a vowel his usage varies. Sometimes he has *–ed,* as in *sued* (I.i.453), *glued* (II.i.41), *vnburied* (I.i.87), *espied* (II.iii.48, 194), *varied* (III.i.81); sometimes *–d* or *–de,* as in *dide* (II. iii.171), *imploid* (IV.iii.39), but on the other hand, *inioyed* (II.iii.22), at the end of a line. It would be difficult to invent a good spelling for the short vowel in the last syllable of *unburied, varied.*

The Quartos show much the same pattern as *Titus.* Thus *Hamlet* has *fortified, cried* and *cride, 2 Henry IV* has *sanctified, MND* has *collied.* After *w* the Quartos usually have *–ed. Hamlet* has *hallowed* (I.i.164) but *bestow'd* (IV.iii.12); besides *LLL* has *swallowed, MND* has *followed, hallowed, 2 Henry IV* has *bestowed.* Verbs in *–ew* have *–ed* as *vnualewed, indewed* (*Hamlet* I.iii.19, IV.vii.180), *vnderualewed* (*MV* II. vii.53, but *vnderualewd* at end of line, I.i.165). Such spellings are important to bear in mind. *2 Henry IV* has *ensinewed* at IV.i.172, which both Dover Wilson [3] and Shaaber [4] think is a misprint, because the meter

[3] John Dover Wilson, New Cambridge Edition of *2 Henry IV* (Cambridge University Press, 1946), p. 117.
[4] Matthias A. Shaaber, Variorum Edition of *2 Henry IV* (Philadelphia and London, J. B. Lippincott Company, 1940), p. 509.

requires *insinew'd*. But this is not a misprint. Shakespeare frequently wrote *–ed* after *w*. It conforms to his usual practice.

–ed reduced to *t* or *d*. All the texts show the same pattern as *Titus,* the form usually showing whether *t* or *d* is to be pronounced. Thus *tradust, incenst (Hamlet), learnt* (*2 Henry IV*), *wipte* (*2 Henry IV*), *bard, dard (Hamlet),* and numerous others in all the texts.

–ed as a separate syllable. It goes without saying that it is Shakespeare's practice to note this, but his editors do not always trust Shakespeare. At the end of the line Shakespeare is especially careful to show whether he wants the syllable elided or pronounced in full. Editors often suit themselves. Thus in *Venus and Adonis* he ends riming lines with *ouer-swayed: obayed* (109:111), *armed:harmed* (625:627), *amazed: gazed* (925:927). The Variorum Edition shows that apparently most editors clip the suffix here. On the other hand, Shakespeare spells *prou'd:lou'd* (608:610), *inrag'd:asswag'd* (317-318), and another set of editors prints the full *–ed*. My observation goes to show that modern editors too often make an arbitrary or capricious change in the spelling that Shakespeare obviously intended.

–ed spelled and not pronounced. Occasionally there are examples of *–ed* after a consonant being written out in full and yet elided (*ticed,* II.iii.92). This may be due to the compositor or it may have been difficult to find an unambiguous spelling for the clipped form. In all the Quartos, as in *Titus,* there are occasional examples of *–ed* spelled in full and not pronounced, as

lined (2 Henry IV I.iii.27). So far as my observation goes, these cases are usually after *r* or *u*. Conversely *'d* is spelled where *—ed* is intended, as *repell'd (Hamlet* II.ii.146: here F has *repulsed* and obviously three syllables were intended).

Ben Jonson indicates elision both in prose and verse. He usually distinguishes between *t* and *d,* as *helpt, crackt, accurst, forc't, grac't, spic't;* but he also has *enforc'd, loos'd, promis'd.* After vowels he has *suppli'd, pied, staid.* After *w* he has *'d,* as *chew'd, hallow'd.* After single consonants he has ambiguous forms, as *tan'd* = tanned, *pul'd* = pulled. Massinger, too, regularly indicates elision, but he does not distinguish *t* and *d.* He has forms like *oppresd, dispensd, kepde, recompencd, taxde.* After vowels he has *tri'ed, denide, pay'd.* After *w* he has *'d,* as *follow'd, swallow'd.* The dramatists had the same end in view, but their methods differed.

2. Shakespeare elides *e* in the verbal ending *—en (threatning,* I.i.134, II.i.4, III.i.224, IV.ii.94; *fastned,* V.iii.183). Here the Quartos show the same trend as *Titus.* Ben Jonson has *open'd, poison'd.* Massinger has *cousninge* but *reckoninge, lesseninge.*

3. Similarly the elision of the vowel in the inflectional ending *—est* is regularly indicated. Thus for the second person singular we have *barst* (I.i.291), *suckst* for *suckedest* (II.iii.144), *holpst* (IV.iv.59) punning with *hope* in the next line, and such forms as *sentst, mightst,* and many others. As in the case of *-ed* we have after *u* or *w* the full spelling, *beleeuest* (V.i.71), *sawest* (V.i.93 at the end of the line), *knowest* (II.i.28).

In the superlative we have *dismalst* (I.i.384), *woefulst* (III.i.290), *proud'st* (IV.iv.26), and especially *gallanst* (I.i.317). It is the same pattern in the Quartos. The contraction is represented in the spelling as closely as possible, as *sweatst* (*2 Henry IV* II.iv.234). Occasionally, as in *Titus*, –*est* is printed in full after *w*, as *knowest* (*Hamlet* V.ii.55), *blowest* (*Lucrece* 884). There are desperate spellings such as *poinst* for *pointest* (*Lucrece* 879) or *foule mouthst* for *foul mouthedest* (*2 Henry IV* II.iv.77) or *pleasantst* (*MA* III.i.26). Such spellings occur in Ben Jonson too (*gallans't* for *gallantest*, and *arrant'st*). But Jonson, unlike Shakespeare, marks elision after *w* as well as after consonants (*saw'st*, *found'st*).

4. The elision of a vowel before *r* gives us the most complicated problem. Here I will take verbs and adjectives together. Verbs ending in –*er* usually show –*red* in inflections, but –*ered* also occurs. It is important at times to note what the Quarto reads, as at V.iii.98:

Were they that murdred our Emperours brother.

Modern editors read *murdered* here against what I think was Shakespeare's intention.

Shakespeare's usage varies or perhaps the compositor interfered. He has *tirde* (II.i.98) and *inspirde* (II.ii.10) at the end of the line. He has *fettred* (II.i.15), *flowred* (V.i.15), *deflowred* (II.iv.26) but *deflowrde* (V.iii.38) at the end of the line, *sequestred* (II.iii.75), *wandred* (II.iii.77), but on the other hand *wonderd* (III.i.135), where some modern editors print *wondred*. He always has *martred* for *martyred* (III.i.81,107).

He makes some interesting differentiations. III.i.113 reads

> Vpon a gathred Lillie almost withered.

Most modern editions, except Neilson and Hill, read *gather'd, wither'd,* but Shakespeare obviously wanted to avoid repeating the same ending. Compare line 885 of *Lucrece* with *smotherst* but *murthrest.* V.iii.69 reads

> Scatterd by winds and high tempestuous gusts

but at 71 we have

> This scattered corne into one mutuall sheaffe.

Here the second *scattered* is an adjective and Shakespeare leaves it with *–ed* in full, although that is against the meter. Modern editors reject this reading. They ought to pay stricter attention to the hints that Shakespeare gives them in his spelling.

Shakespeare is consistent in always spelling *–ed* in full after *–our,* as *culloured* (II.iii.83), *honoured* (I.i.245, 427), *dishonoured* (I.i.385, 425). It is noticeable that he spells *checkerd,* in a *checkerd shadow* (II.iii.15).

Before *–ing* he usually notices the elision (*lingring,* II.i.110), but at II.iii.39 he has

> Blood and reuenge are hammering in my head.

Surely the elision in this line is avoided with intention. In the second person singular he has *sufferst* (I.i.87) but *thundrest* (II.i.58).

Adjectives ending in *–arous, –erous, –orous* usually do not show elision (*barbarous, –erous,* II.iii.118,

V.i.97, iii.4; *murderous, murtherous,* II.iii.267,
IV.ii.88; *treacherous,* IV.ii.117; *traiterous, –orous,*
I.i.302, 452, IV.i.93, IV.53). On the other hand, you
have *wondrous* (II.iii.112), which, if it is formed on
wonders (see *NED*), may never have been trisyllabic.
Adventrous (V.iii.112) goes back deep into Middle
English, and later Marvell was to use it (*Horatian Ode*
11) and Pope (*Rape of the Lock* II.26, III.29). We have
also *flattrie* (III.1.254), *watrie* (III.i.269) and *uttrance*
(V.iii.91).

The Quartos show the same variation as *Titus*. In
verbal endings the *e* is usually elided. Thus *Hamlet* has
*incountred, vngartred, remembred, suffring, swag-
gring.* On the other hand, *Hamlet* has *liuer'd, labour'd,*
and always *honour'd.* When the *–ed* is added to a noun
Hamlet has *beggerd* (IV.v.92), *fingard* (V.ii.15),
siluer'd (I.ii.243). In a number of cases all the texts
print *–ed* in full against the meter; for instance, *Hamlet* has *deliuered* (I.ii.209), *nabored* (II.ii.12), *considered* as an adjective (II.ii.81), and *2 Henry IV* has *ventured* (I.i.183), where F₁ has *ventur'd. Hamlet* has one
delicious example of a pronunciation-spelling:

Oremastret as you may (I.v.140; F₁ *O'remaster't;* Q₁
Or emaister it).

In nouns and adjectives *Hamlet* like *Titus* has *uttrance*
(III.ii.378), also *Nunry* (III.i.122–142), *cronet weeds*
(IV.vii.173), *boystrous* (III.iii.22), *desprat* (IV.vii.26),
sulphrus (I.v.3). *MND* has *Votresse* (II.i.123, 163),
watry (I.i.210, II.i.162, III.i.203), *lethren* (II.ii.4).
Wondrous is common in all the texts. *LLL* has *foolrie*

(IV.iii.163, V.ii.76). *MV* has *lottrie* both in prose and verse (I.ii.31, II.i.15) and *waterie, watry* in poetry (II.vii.44, III.ii.47). *Hamlet* has *leaprous* (I.v.64), where the meter demands three syllables.

Notice Shylock's

For suffrance is the badge of all our Trybe (I. iii. 111)

but *sufferance* in prose (III.i.73). There are numerous cases where elision is not marked, as in Hamlet's *trecherous, lecherous . . . villain* (II.ii.609), *aduenterous* (II.ii.333 in prose), *dangerous* (III.i.4), *vlcerous* (III. iv.147). *Souereignty* is generally elided in pronunciation but rarely in spelling except once in *Lucrece*, which reads

Perchance his bost of Lucrece Sou'raigntie (l. 36)

—and then most modern editors print the full form!

In the *Merchant of Venice* there occurs a threefold spelling of *interest:*

> *Ant.* And what of him, did he take interrest?
> *Shyl.* No, not take interest, not as you would say
>   Directly intrest, marke what Iacob did. (I. iii. 76–8)

Intrest occurs again in III.ii.224. No one will convince me that Shakespeare did not intend *trecherous, lecherous* to have three syllables or each of these three spellings of *interest* to convey a meaning. Again we see Shakespeare having his fun with language, again we hear his very accents.

There is a most important passage in the *Merchant of Venice*. Portia devises a song for Bassanio

"Tell me where is fancie bred"

and in the middle of it plumps the clumsy word *en-gendred*. It is like putting an elephant in a canoe. Every editor of Shakespeare ought to be trained to print Shakespeare's form; those who print it as *en-gender'd* of course destroy the reason for its existence. Editors make a great mistake at 2 *Henry IV* IV.iv.99 which reads

> Are by the shrieue of Yorkshire ouerthrowne.

The Folio reads *Sherife*, murdering the line, and nearly all modern editors follow it, with the notable exception of Dover Wilson, who restores the Quarto form.

Ben Jonson usually prefers *–r'd* (*alter'd, gather'd, scatter'd, honour'd*) but he has *remembred* and *hungred*. In the adjective he nearly always marks elision (*boistrous, perj'rous, ulc'rous,* but *sulphurous*). He also has *cor'siue* for *corrosive* and he likes to write *yond'* for *yonder*. Massinger regularly has *–r'd* (*enter'd, fetter'd, honor'd*). Once he has *accoutred*. In the present participle he elides (*suffring, tendring*).

5. Verbs ending in *–le* spell the participle and preterite *–led* (*dissembled, humbled, mangled*). Participles ending in *–len* are frequently contracted to one syllable (*bigswolne,* III.i.224). On the other hand, at II.iii.198, Q_1 reads:

> Why art thou fallen what subtill hole is this.

Most modern editions—but not Neilson and Hill—read *fall'n,* but surely the dissyllable is intended. In this line we have a tragic question followed by a pause of horror.

The Quartos agree with *Titus*. Thus *Hamlet* has *iangled, setled, sickled, vnhuzled, iugled* (IV.v.130, where the Folio has *Iuggel'd*). Other forms occur, as *grissl'd, metteld* (*Hamlet* I.ii.240, II.ii.594), *enammeld* (*MND* II.i.255), *pencel'd* (*Lucrece* 1497). *Enammeld, metteld, penceld* are to be explained by the parallel noun-form. In the strong past participle we have *falne* (*Hamlet, MA*), *stolne* (2 *Henry IV, MA, MND, LLL, Lucrece*), *swolne* (2 *Henry IV, Venus*).

Ben Jonson has *dazeled, setled, wrinckled* and *stol'ne*. Massinger has *doublde, croniclde, manaclde*. It is possible that Massinger was indicating by his spelling a pronunciation like the modern one, while Shakespeare and Ben Jonson may have said *set-led*. Massinger also has *swolne*.

6. Then there is the clipping of *l, s, t, th* in tiny words like *has, his, is, it, the, to, will. Titus* has its fill of these, as *let's, shee's, was't* = was it, *wilt please you* = will it please you, *t'appease, th'infernall, thou'st* = thou hast, *Ile, youle, weele, thoult,* and many more. At one place the compositor, trying to save space, prints *Ile* where only *I will* is possible.

    So now bring them in for Ile play the Cooke (V. ii. 205).

So is extrametrical. The line should read:

    So/Now bring them in for I will play the cook.

Modern editions read *I'll*. The compositor makes the opposite mistake at IV.i.101:

    You are a young huntsman *Marcus,* let alone.

Here *You are* should be read *You're. Let alone* stands for *let it alone* and is so printed in Q³. Compare *le't not be doubted,* for *let it not be doubted (Winter's Tale* II.ii.63, and the long note on II.i.18 in Furness's Variorum Edition of this play, p. 91).

These abbreviations are common forms in Elizabethan. They are of course frequent in the Quartos. I doubt if anything is so characteristic of a writer's orthography as the range of abbreviations that he prefers. Ben Jonson's are not Shakespeare's; he likes *'hem (taxe 'hem), do'not* = don't, *ha' (I'ld ha' desir'd you), euer sin' yesterday noone, gi' him not the head.* Massinger is very fond of *'em (studie 'em, from 'em);* he has not so many abbreviations as Shakespeare or Ben Jonson.

7. Finally we come to the elision of a medial weak vowel standing between two syllables, one with the chief accent, the other with a secondary accent.

Let him receaue no sustnance, fetter him. (V. iii. 6)

This kind of elision occurs in the Quartos, thus *medcin (Hamlet* V.ii.325, Folio *Medicine), medcine (MND* III.ii.264, Folio *medicine), medcine (2 Henry IV* IV.v.163, Folio *Med'cine),* but *medicine (Romeo and Juliet* II.iii.24), although it is a dissyllable there. In prose we have *medcinable (MA* II.ii.5). *Hamlet* also has *ordnance* (V.ii.281, Folio *Ordinance).* Ben Jonson has *rau'nous* for *ravenous* but *Ordinance.* Massinger has *ravenous.*

II

1. The second group, the phonetic spellings as I have called them, is extremely interesting. Here we see the Elizabethans so intent on spelling the word as it is

pronounced that they disregard etymology entirely. For instance, they doubled the consonant after a short vowel in the accented syllable of dissyllables and polysyllables. So Shakespeare spells *cabbin, cittie, commeth, intollerable, maddam, Nobillitie, plannet, pollicie, tyrranize,* and very many others. The Quartos are full of similar spellings, which indeed may be found in any Elizabethan book. Shakespeare may also double the consonant after the unstressed syllable—*mellodious, sollicite.* Ben Jonson of course has these spellings, too, but not nearly so many as Shakespeare. He has *Pattent, forraine, choller, scholler, corollarie,* but *abilitie, qualified, quality, polititian, merit, tyranous,* and many other cases of a single consonant after a short vowel. In Massinger it is the same: he gives us *relligion, relligious, callamity* (in these cases in the unstressed syllable), *skelliton, Pallace,* but *malice, policie, madam, senate, tyrannie, tyrannous.* Shakespeare is much more thorough than either Jonson or Massinger in indicating the shortness of the vowel in this position.

2. Probably pronunciation also explains Shakespeare's treatment of weak, unaccented vowels. He gets them all mixed up. He is fond of reducing *i, o, u* to *e.* Thus we have *Batchiler, enmetie, gratefie, ideot, mightenes, priueledge, prodegies, Sibels, testemonie, tortering, venemous.* Weak *e* becomes *i,* as in *mistris* and *inough.* Initial *des–* is spelled *dis–,* as in *discipher'd, dispaire, dispightfull, dispisde.* In one case weak *o* becomes *a* (*promontarie*) and *e* becomes *a* (*apparant*) and *o* (*tapors*).

Such spellings are common in the Quartos. Jonson

and Massinger use them, but much less frequently than Shakespeare. Jonson especially fills his play with a profusion of polysyllabic words where it would be easy to go wrong. But he spells them strictly according to etymology. Shakespeare, on the other hand, was chiefly interested in rendering pronunciation.

3. We now come to spellings that no doubt represent pronunciation in some cases, but as the ground for Shakespeare's preference is not always clear, I group them all together—*ai* in final syllables (*battailes* I.i.66, but *Battleaxe,* III.i.169; *sodaine,* I.i.318, 393; *Romaines,* I.i.9, frequent; *Romane,* I.i.322, II.i.113; *Romans,* I.i.257, short line that could well accommodate *Romaines*). Such spellings occur in the Quartos; *counsaile* is frequent, *suddaine* (*Hamlet* IV.vii.47), *Romaine, Romane* (2 *Henry IV* II.ii.135, *Hamlet* V.ii.352, *Lucrece* 51, 505). Jonson has *suddaine, travaile.* Massinger has *battaile, counsaile, suddaine* but always *Roman.*

4. *au* before *n + c, ch, s, t, d* (*chaunces, raunsomes, aduaunce, auntient, commaund, daunst, infraunchised,* and many more), but before *–ng–* only *a* (*change, dangerous*). Of course this difference is based on a difference of pronunciation. The Quartos show much the same pattern as *Titus.* Jonson has *commaund, daunce, chaunce,* and *chance.* Before *–ng–* he has *change, chaunge, daunger, strange, straunge.* Massinger has a straight *a* all through, *advance, avant, chant, danger, lance.*

5. *ai, ay* in final syllables (*waid,* I.i.55; *wayd,* 73; *pray* = prey, III.i.55, IV.ii.96, V.iii.198; *suruay,* I.i.

446). *Pray, wayd,* and the like, are common in the Quartos. Jonson has *outwai'd* and Massinger has *waigh.*

6. *im–, in–* (*imbrace, –ment, imploid, inchaunt, infraunchise, inuiron,* but *encamp, enquire* on the same page, I4b).

The spellings with *im–, in–* are very frequent in *Titus*. In the Quartos they are far more frequent than *em–, en–.* Jonson has *intreat,* but *embrac'd.* Massinger has *embrace* but *incrochinge, ingag'd, inioy* and many others.

7. *l* before a final consonant is single (*els, smels, distild, cald*). This is common Elizabethan.

8. *o* before *l* is usually *ou, ow* (*rowle, skrowle* but *scrole, controwl* but *controlde*). This is no doubt a spelling pronunciation. The usage in the Quartos varies, *ou–, ow–* being the usual form. Jonson has *controuling.* Massinger has *behould, scrowle.*

9. *s* in *–less, –ness* is usually single (*humblenes*). *Hamlet* shows the same tendency. This is a spelling where the compositor was free to choose his letters to space the line, so that only the regularity of it makes it valid as a clue. It is remarkable, too, that Jonson and Massinger have comparatively few cases of *–les* and *–nes.*

10. *s, sc. Sythia,* I.i.131; *semitars,* IV.ii.91; but *Bascianus* 10 times, *Bassianus* 5 times; *Silence* with *s,* I.i.90, 155, II.iii.33. In the Quartos we have *Symitar* (*MV* II.i.24), *sythe* (*LLL* I.i.6).

11. *t, c* in suffixes. *Titus* has *gratious* 15 times, also *ambitiously, pretious, spatious, suspition, auntient, patience, impatient.* No other Quarto is so consistent.

Hamlet, for instance, has *gracious, gratious, spacious, auncient, auspitious, impatient.* Jonson has *impatient, malitious, Polititian, physitian* and *physician, pretious* but *spacious.* Massinger has *gratious, Patritian, pretious, spetial, spetious, pacyence.* Of course the similarity of *t* and *c* in Elizabethan script accounts for some of this confusion.

12. I now give a list of single words with a special spelling that appears to be characteristic of Shakespeare:

atchiue (II.i.80,106); compare *MV* III.ii.210, *MA* I.i.8.

ceaze = seize (I.i.405, IV.ii.96), also *Venus* 25, 158, 697; *seaz'd* (*Hamlet* I.i.89). In Jonson.

cote = quote (IV.i.50). Frequent in the Quartos.

despight (also *spight, wright* = write). Such spellings frequent in the Quartos.

diuel = devil. So also in Quartos.

hart and *heart* vary. So in Quartos.

I = ay. So in Quartos.

loose = lose. Frequent in Quartos. In Jonson and Massinger.

murther more common than *murder.* So in Quartos. *Venus* rhymes *murther: further* (905–6).

president = precedent (V.iii.44). So in *MV* IV.i.220, *Hamlet* V.ii.260. Also in Jonson and Massinger.

renowmed, V.i.20 (*renowned,* I.i.38). Also in *Romeo and Juliet* III.v.62.

then = than. Everywhere in the Quartos.

vertue. Everywhere in the Quartos. In Jonson and Massinger.

vilde = vile. Everywhere in the Quartos.

yeeld. Everywhere in the Quartos.

All of these spellings occur more or less frequently outside Shakespeare; they are not unique. But Shakespeare's liking for them is another link between *Titus* and the Quartos.

13. There is one peculiarity of spelling, fairly frequent in the Quartos, that we do not find in *Titus*. The other Quartos show a remarkable number of words ending in *–ique* (*antique, musique, politique, publique, traffique*). *Titus* spells *musicke* (II.i.70) and it does not show *–ique* anywhere. *Hamlet* has *hectique, publique; MA* has *heretique, politique; LLL* has *publique, frantique, lunatique, antique* and various spellings of *rhetoric* with the ending in *–cke, –ike, –ique.* The spelling of *music* varies from play to play. On the whole it appears as if Shakespeare preferred to spell this ending *ique.*

14. *Titus* is a Roman play full of classical names and Latin words which are consistently misspelled. We have *Acaron* (IV.iii.44; but *Acheron* in *MND* III.ii.357), *Andronicy* (I.i, in the cut passage) and *Andronicie* (V.iii.131), *Ayax* (I.i.379), *Capitoll* (I.i.12, 77) but *Capitall* (I.i.41), *Epeons* for *Hyperions* (V.ii.56), *Ocitus* for *Cocytus* (II.iii.236), *Panthean* (I.i.333), *Pathan* (I.i.242), *Semirimis* and *Semeramis* (II.i.22, II.iii.118), *Tytus* for *Titans* (I.i.226), and *suum cuiqum* for *suum cuique* (I.i.280), *Ad manus fratrum* for *. . . manes . . .* (I.i.98). At first sight it would appear that the copy for *Titus* was written by a person whose Latin was very "small." Typically *Epeons* for

Hyperions suggests rather that the writing was difficult to decipher and that the compositor was helpless when confronted by classical words that he did not know. He just stabbed at the word with a frantic guess. *Pathan* and *Panthean* have never been satisfactorily explained. Both the large number of bad spellings and their preposterousness make it certain that Shakespeare did not read the proofs of *Titus*.

One spelling, however, is neither a mistake nor a misprint. Shakespeare gets some fun out of the form *Iubiter* for *Iupiter* in IV.iii. He prepares us for his mischief by making Marcus say:

> Your letter is with Iubiter by this. (1. 66)

After this the Clown comes in and Titus says:

> Shall I have iustice, what saies Iubiter (1. 78),

to which the Clown replies:

> Ho the Gibbet-maker?

Shakespeare works up to his pun carefully. Q₂ and all subsequent editions spoil Shakespeare's joke by printing *Jupiter*. However, *Iubiter* is a good Middle English form (compare *debuty, jeobardy* for *deputy, jeopardy*), but so far as I know Shakespeare is the only writer to use it in the late sixteenth century. It is another example of how much he knew about English words.

With regard to Latin words and names I have not found any text that was so full of mistakes as *Titus*. Occasionally we get apparent pronunciation-spellings of foreign names, as *King Couetua* for *Cophetua*

(2 *Henry IV* V.iii.106, Folio *Couitha*). But this is
Pistol's English and I think Shakespeare intended
Pistol to mispronounce the word.

15. I have left out of consideration certain spellings
that Professor Dover Wilson considers important, for
instance, "the absence of e mute," as in *safty, whol-
some, associat* and other words. We must remember
that the compositor reserved to himself full liberty to
add or drop *e*.

Dr. A. W. Pollard notes that "most printers would
add *e* to any possible word, or knock it out, or possibly
even add or omit an *u* or *h* in a word like guest in order
to help the spacing. . . . [In the 1611 edition of the
Bible] the only consistency is that the form is always
preferred which suits the spacing." [5]

In any case it is a general Elizabethan trend to drop
e before a suffix. Thus *Titus* has *housholds* (V.iii.
194).

With regard to *associat* it is true that *Hamlet* has
–at, –it more frequently than *–ate, –ite*. In *Titus* and in
2 Henry IV on the other hand, *–ate, –ite* are the regular
spellings, and in the other Quartos they appear to be
rather more numerous than *–at, –it*. Before *–ly* the *e* is
dropped—*immediatly* (*Titus*), *temperatly* (*Hamlet*),
immoderatly (*LLL*), *immedeatlie, priuatly* (*MV*).
That is in accordance with the trend to drop final *e*
before a suffix.

[5] Alfred W. Pollard, "Elizabethan Spelling as a Bibliographical Clue,"
The Library, 4th Ser., IV (1923), 5–6. See also my *History of Ablaut
in the Strong Verbs*, Bonner Studien zur Englischen Philologie, III
(1910), 1–2.

III

The two poems *Venus and Adonis* and the *Rape of Lucrece* are probably closer to Shakespeare than any of the Quartos. He would no doubt read the manuscript through carefully before letting the printer have it, and he certainly corrected the proofs. On the whole the spelling is the same as in the other Quartos, except that the weak vowels are more "correctly" or less phonetically spelled.[6] For instance, in *prodigies* we have *i,* not the *e* of the Quartos. We also have *mistresse,* not *mistris.*

The ending *–ique* occurs only once (*reumatique,* 135), otherwise *frantikely* (1059), *musick.* We have *colourd* (1) instead of *culloured* as in *Titus.* These spellings show a tendency to normalize. As the book was dedicated to Southampton and no doubt formally presented to him, Shakespeare would have every reason to be careful about matters of correctness. At the same time Shakespeare keeps several of his old customs; he has:

ai in *convaide.*
ay in *pray = prey, obay.*
au in *daunce,* etc.
c, t in *suspition, dissention, dissentious,* but *sacietie.*
im–, in– in *imbracement, infold,* but *enfranchising.*
l single in *ful, dwels, swolne, cald.*
Inflectional *–ed* is written *d* or *t* according to pronunciation, but more often with the apostrophe. However,

6 See also Wilhelm Marschall, "Shakespeares Orthographie," *Anglia* LI (1927), 307–322.

occasionally a *d* is written for *t* (*pale-fac'd,* 569, but
black-fac't, 773). After a vowel or *w,* the *ed* is sometimes
written in full—*thawed* (749), *wooed* (97, 358), *swayed:
obayed* (109:111 in rhyme), but *bestow'd* (77), *dew'd*
(66). Verbs ending in *–er* are spelled with *–red* or
–erd: checkred (1168), *murdred* (502), *feathred* (306),
gathred (131), *battred* (104), *tired* (177), but *maisterd*
(392), *betterd* (78), *temperd* (3 times), *sufferd* (388).
Master, better, temper have parallels as nouns or adjectives and *sufferd* is normal in Shakespeare. The
nouns give *intrest* (210), *flattry:battry* (rhyme 425–26);
and in the adjective we have *boystrous* (326), but also
timerous (35, 88). This mixture is sufficiently like what
you find in the Quartos. Special words, *ceazeth* (25),
curtsie (888), *despight, president* (26), *then* (= than),
vertue (1131), follow the usage of *Titus;* but *heart* and
loseth (420) are instances of normal correct spellings,
not usual in *Titus.*

Venus and Adonis shows enough similarity with the
Quartos in general and with *Titus* in particular to
make it plausible that both texts come from a manuscript very near to Shakespeare.

The *Rape of Lucrece* shows the same general char-
acteristics as *Venus.* It is only necessary to remark on
one or two notable spellings. Like *Titus* it has the
forms *Romaine* (505), *battaile* (145), *ceazd* (677), *cote*
(812), *despight, loose, murther, vertue, yeeld.* On the
other hand, it has *deuill* not *diuill,* and both *heart* and
hart. Its weak vowels are usually more "correct," as
hither, mistress, priuiledge, and many more, as against
deuine, dispaire, lechors, accessarie. In the suffix *–ed*

we have the forms *borrowed* (573, 1549), *vnhallowed* (392), *shadowed* (1416), but at the end of the line, *thawd* (884); these we know from *Titus*. There are a good many apostrophes, some confusing, as *lim'd* for *limed* (88) with *dim'd* for *dimmed* (448). The distinction is kept between voiced and voiceless consonants; thus we have *leapt, perplext, fortrest, triumpht, slakt, forst* = forced, *inforst* = enforced, but *black-fac'd* (1518). After *–er* the elision is sometimes not noted, as in the adjectives *conquered* (482), *slaughtered* (188); otherwise *hammerd, sepulcherd, labour'd, attir'd, shiuer'd,* but also the adjectives *slaughtred* (1376, 1733), *sugred* (893), the verb *maistred* (863), *smothred* (adjective, 783) and *smotherd* (verb, 418). There is a triple rhyme *desired, tyred, admyred* (415–418), which, according to the Variorum Edition, modern editors smother in a triple apostrophe. *Tired* occurs again as two syllables (1617). There are the nouns and adjectives *intrest* (1067), *interest* (1797, two syllables), *waterie, watrie* (1748,1745), *desp'rat* (1038), but *desperat* (739, two syllables), *sou'raigntie* (36), *soueraignty* (69). At 802 we have *martird*, not *martred* as in *Titus*. Before *–est* elision is not shown after a vowel or *w* (*seest,* 322; *blowest,* 884), although it is generally marked in other cases (*quiuerst, gau'st, graunt'st, murthrest,* but *makest,* 883). In the present participle we have *blustring, ventring.*

A study of the Variorum Edition of these two poems shows that editors still have a lot to learn about the editing of Shakespeare. They consistently ignore Shakespeare's indication of rhythm and they contrast

or expand the elided syllables as seems fit to them—
not to Shakespeare.

Taking all these spellings together, we find the same
general pattern as in *Titus* and the Quartos. No text is
altogether consistent with itself nor does any text re-
semble the general pattern in every detail. But there
is enough general likeness to support the theory that
these Quartos all belong to one family. The ground for
their resemblance to one another which makes them a
family is that they are printed from the same kind of
copy, which was a manuscript written by Shakespeare
himself. To this family of texts we have every right to
add *Titus Andronicus*.

From all these details there emerges a very clear picture of Shakespeare at work. We knew before that
Shakespeare was interested in words, but till you study
his spellings you do not know what a lot of fun Shakespeare got out of language. Throughout Q_1 you see
him marking elisions and contractions and scorning
etymology and tradition in order to pin down the
word to its pronunciation. It is almost as if we heard
his voice over our shoulders.

We get exactly the same impression from a study of
Shakespeare's prose, but unfortunately there is not
enough prose in *Titus* on which to form a judgment.
The joke with *Iubiter,* however, is typical of how
Shakespeare's intentions are obscured in our modern
editions. Shakespeare gets fun out of language in various ways. Quickly's idiosyncrasies serve to accentuate
her quality, as an illiterate, feckless, helpless woman, a

natural prey for Falstaff. *Wheeson* for *Whetsun* or *Peesell* for *Pistol, Wedsday* for *Wednesday,* surely these fumblings give us the woman. And especially *debuty* for *deputy*. Does not that pronunciation give us all the woman's rich, fat greasiness? Again when Falstaff speaks of the "Jarman" hunting in waterwork (*2 Henry IV* II.i.157), a certain racy tone comes into his prose that is quite lost in our modern spelling "German." When Silence speaks of his daughter as a "woosel," we print *ousel,* and lose the suggestion of a Farmer Hayseed speaking dialect. Our modern editions ought to pay more attention to Shakespeare's fun. He does not overdo colloquial, regional, or illiterate pronunciations; they just serve to enliven dialogue here and there. The more's the pity that our modern editions eliminate them altogether.

Since *Titus* unfortunately has no long passages of prose, it is impossible to state from the Quarto the parallelism that exists between Shakespeare's use in verse and prose. I have a confession to make. I used to be so simple as to think somewhere at the back of my mind that the contractions and elisions we find in Shakespeare's verse formed a kind of poetic license. I ought to have realized that his prose was just as much clipped as his poetry. It shows all the characteristic shortenings. Now, in verse our modern editions will mark with an apostrophe every syllable that is shortened, as, for instance, *lov'd* for *loved,* but in prose they tend to print all such forms in full. Shakespeare, however, writes the same language in prose as in poetry. Our modern printing conventions conceal from us a certain unity of style which holds a Shakespearean play together. Moreover, unless we recognize that Shakespeare writes poetry and prose in the same convention, we shall not realize to the full the freshness, spontaneity, and vigor of his verse.

Ben Jonson and Massinger are trying to do the same thing as Shakespeare, but each in a different fashion. In some ways Jonson goes further than Shakespeare, for instance, in using forms like *perj'rous, ulc'rous* or in docking the smaller parts of speech. But on the whole Shakespeare is closer than Jonson to actual pronunciation. He is much closer than Massinger, who has unpronounceable forms like *kepd.* Massinger has several idiosyncrasies like *buisnesse, gieue, cowlde, showlde, wowlde,* and *æ* in Latin words like *æqualls, fælicitie, quæstion.*

M. St. Clare Byrne has investigated Munday's spelling "as a literary clue."[7] She finds the use of the double medial vowel (*affoord, woorship*) is consistent throughout (p. 11), and she shows that it is not the work of the compositor. "In no text printed by Charlwood that I have been able to examine have I found the *–oo* form used consistently" (p. 15).

It is clear that Jonson, Massinger, and Munday had their idiosyncrasies which set them off from other writers and, of course, from Shakespeare. I think it is equally clear that Shakespeare is also distinguished by idiosyncrasies that are not mere preferences for one set of letters over another. They are rooted in a habit

[7] Muriel St. Clare Byrne, "Anthony Munday's Spelling as a Literary Clue," *The Library,* 4th Ser., IV (1923), 9–23.

of thought which shows itself especially in Shakespeare's methodical attempt to get as near the pronunciation as possible.

If we remember that Shakespeare deliberately shaped spelling to indicate the pronunciations he desired, then the authentic texts, both prose and verse, when rightly studied, come to life with an unexpected freshness and beauty. Some questions still remain obscure. Presumably—we do not know—Shakespeare wrote *growest, followed,* instead of *grow'st, follow'd,* because he wanted the words pronounced that way. When he wrote:

> So hallowed, and so gratious is that time,

it is legitimate to infer that he preferred the rhythm of *hallowed* to *hallow'd.* He may have been thinking of what he heard at every church-service, *Hallowéd be thy name.* One thing is certain: these spellings frequently reveal Shakespeare's fine ear and his love of delicate rhythm. In endings like *–ar–, –or–, –erous,* his elisions are easy to pronounce. And where he does not elide, it is for the delicacy of the rhythm. He avoids the ugly clumsiness of such elisions as Jonson's *perj'rous.*

Modern scholars like Kittredge, Neilson, and Dover Wilson are gradually revealing to us the beauty of Shakespeare's line. Not enough justice has been done to the aesthetic values of scholarship. Scholars are supposed to have souls as hard as shoe leather and to pay attention to matters like spelling because poetry is beyond their reach. Actors sneer at us as if we were moles blindly working in the dark, and the aesthetic critics sniff when we come near them. And yet we few, we happy few, we band of brothers, are the only people who know how to read Shakespeare; to us alone is his rare and refreshing fruit really sweet and juicy. We are like Saul, the son of Kish, who went out to seek his father's asses and who found a kingdom. If the actors and the aesthetes want to find that kingdom too, they had better join us, or they will never get there.

Copyright of Plays in
the Early Seventeenth Century

꿎

By GILES E. DAWSON

COPYRIGHT as we know it today is a complex system of statutory law. It not only covers books, but provides special protections for such diverse forms of composition as sheet music, moving pictures, and billboard advertisements.

The development of the modern concept of copyright has been a slow one. An important milestone of that development was the enactment of the first copyright statute, which became effective on the tenth day of April 1710. The statute was entitled

An Act for the Encouragment of learning by Vesting
the Copies of Printed Books in the Authors or Purchasers
of such Copies, during the Times therein mentioned.

There are two points here worthy of notice. One is that authors of books are particularly mentioned, and certain provisions of the Act are designed to protect them against exploitation by publishers. The other is that in neither the title nor the body of the statute is the word "copyright" used. The first appearance of this word in print that has come to my attention is in

1734.[1] In the Act, and for many years before it, the word "copy" was used with a meaning almost indistinguishable from that which we call "copyright." For though the word had not come into use, the concept was by no means new in 1710, and now it is customary to refer to it as "copyright" even when speaking of an earlier period, as I shall do here.

The legal proposition that a man is entitled to the fruits of his labor is a very old one—older than the art of printing. It was the application of this principle to printed books which led to the few known instances of privilege granted to authors or publishers by princes or states as early as the fifteenth century. But in the early years of printing, the market was limited, printers were few, and what demand there was was chiefly for standard works of theology or classical literature. Therefore a unified system of copyright was hardly needed, and the machinery for enforcing such rights as were recognized was not developed until well into the sixteenth century.

But as literacy increased, and printers became more numerous, competition for the growing market became keener, and the need arose for various kinds of regulation of the trade. It may safely be said that even before the incorporation of the Stationers' Company some reasonably efficient steps must have been taken to protect literary property. It would soon have become apparent to those who invested capital in the

[1] In an "advertisement" appended to a 1734 edition of *The Merry Wives*, where Jacob Tonson, the publisher, speaks of "the Proprietors of the Copy-Right."

publication of books, that without at least limited protection against uncontrolled reprinting, no investment
was safe. The natural protectors of literary property
were the several guilds connected with book production and distribution, for their chief function was the
regulation of trade in a manner advantageous to all
their members.

In 1557 the Company of Stationers of London was
incorporated by royal charter. Though the stationers
favored such incorporation—which greatly increased
their powers and assured them of a monopoly—the
initiative was taken by the Crown. The authorities saw
in it a means of more effectively and more easily controlling the output of the press in a politically disturbed period. The Stationers' Company was to share
with the ecclesiastical and civil authorities the responsibility for censorship, though plays, which had previously given much offense, were still to be subject to
the licensing power of the Archbishop of Canterbury,
the Bishop of London, and their deputies. In the exercise of their other function—of regulating their own
trade—the stationers were greatly strengthened. The
charter enabled them to enforce the monopoly which
it created, by granting them power to search for illegal
presses and to seize or destroy them. And, what is of
more importance for the present discussion, it em-
powered them to make ordinances and to enforce
them by fines and imprisonment. As part of the machinery for carrying out its functions, the Company
kept a Hall Book, now known as the Stationers' Register. Here the clerk entered all matters of interest—

miscellaneous expenses, the articling of apprentices, fines and other punishments, the licenses to print books, and so forth. For the first twenty years, the Hall Book was not kept in a very careful manner. But after about 1580, records relating to books became fairly systematic.

It is these entries that concern us in the investigation of copyright. For copyright was—and for about a century remained—nothing but a system of rules developed and enforced by the Stationers' Company to regulate the trade for the benefit of its members.

There is one exception. A kind of copyright which had little to do with the Stationers' Company is privilege granted by royal patent. Law books, Bibles, grammars, music books, and certain other classes of books, and even a few individual books, were—for periods of varying length—so protected. But these, though constituting no inconsiderable part of the bulk of printed books, are exceptions. This system of privilege looks backward to the medieval way of government rather than ahead to statutory copyright. And it is not the system of copyright which ordinarily applied to plays.

For copyright within the Stationers' Company, virtually all information must come from two sources—the registers and court books of the company, and the imprints of the books themselves. If we did not have the Stationers' Register, we could still infer from the imprints a good deal about ownership of copies, but we should know little about how copyright worked—how a claim was established and how it passed from bookseller to bookseller. Most of what we know about these processes comes from the Stationers' Register. It will be well then to consider for a few moments the various forms of book entries in the Register and their meanings in relation to copyright.

The earliest entries, up to 1588, usually take some such form as

> Received of Thomas colwell for his lycense for pryntinge of ye playe of susanna [1569] [2]

or

> **Roger ward** Lycensed vnto him an enterlude intituled all for money. [1577]

These sound as if the Stationers' Company were in each case actually licensing a play—placing their stamp of approval on it and assuming responsibility to the government "that nothing therein [was] . . . heretical, seditious, or unseemly for Christian ears." At times they undoubtedly did exercise this function. And perhaps these entries imply, or include, such approval of the contents. But we must not be misled by the word "license" into supposing that such is necessarily the case. An entry of 1582 throws light on the use of this word:

> **John Charlewood** Receaved of him for his licence to printe theis Copies hereafter mencõned. . . . Alwaies provided That yf it be founde that anie other hath righte to printe anie of theis Copies, That then this his

[2] This and all subsequent extracts from the Stationers' Register are, except as otherwise indicated, quoted from W. W. Greg, *Bibliography of the English Drama to the Restoration* (Bibliographical Soc.), I (1939), where (pp. 1–76) Greg prints all entries relating to plays. Since Greg's entries are arranged chronologically and I supply a date for each quotation, I have considered further references unnecessary.

> lycence as touchinge euerie suche of those Copies soe be-
> longinge to anie other shalbe void and of none effecte.
> . . . Copies wch were Sampson Awdeleys and nowe ly-
> cenced to the said Iohn Charlewood vnder the con-
> dicõn aforesaid. . . .

In spite of the constant use of the word "license," this
is a record of transfer, and the so-called "license to
print" is simply the company's official recognition of
Charlewood's right as against other members of the
company. In short it is a transfer of copyright. In 1584
a play is entered to Thomas Cadman thus:

> Yt is graunted vnto him y^t if he gett ye comedie of sappho
> laufully alowed vnto him. Then none of this cumpanie
> shall Interrupt him to enioye yt.

Here the Stationers' Company specifically refused to
accept responsibility for censorship. Perhaps something in the play—though it is not easy to guess what
—was thought to be possibly objectionable; at any
rate, with or without proper allowance, the play was
printed for Cadman in the same year. After this date
it is common for book entries to contain the name of
a licenser—most often the Bishop of London or one
of his Domestic Chaplains, his deputies.

The entries which I have so far quoted have been of
two sorts, both of common occurrence throughout the
seventeenth century. One sort recorded the transfer of
copies from one owner to another. The others were initial entries of new books. After 1588 the word "license" disappears, and initial entries usually take the
form

Richard Jones. Entered for his copy . . .

It now seems clear that the main function of entries in the Register was to record the ownership of copyright. About 1620 the bookseller John Bill wrote that

this entry in ye hall booke is the commun and strongest assurance yat Stationers haue, for all their copies.[3]

Again, the Ordinances of the company of 1681 state that

by ancient Usage of this Company, when any Book or Copy is duly Entred in the Register Book of this Company, to any Member or Members . . . such Person to whom such Entry is made, is, and always hath been reputed and taken to be Proprietor of such Book or Copy, and ought to have the sole Printing thereof.[4]

An entry of 18 December 1592 demonstrates the practical value of entry in the Hall Book:

Yt is ordered: that if the book of Dĉor ffaustus [not the play] shall not be found in the hall book entred to Richard Oliff before Abell Ieffes claymed the same wch was about May last. That then the seid copie shall Remayne to the said Abell as his prop*er* copie. . . .

From John Bill's statement and the ruling over *Doctor Faustus,* it might appear that entrance in the Book was all that was required. But several typical entries will show that such was not the case:

28 m*a*rcij [1600]
Cutbert Burby Entred for his copie vnder the hand*es* of the Wardens. The Plaie of Patient Grissell.

xiij Maij [1606] . . .
Iohn Trundell Iohn Busbye Entred for their Copie by warrant from Mr Norton vnder his hand A Comedie

[3] Edward Arber, *Transcript of the Registers of the Company of Stationers of London, 1554–1640* (1875–94), III, 39.   [4] *Ibid.,* I, 22.

called The Fleare. provided that they are not to printe
yt tell they bringe good aucthoritie and licence for the
doinge thereof.

Almost every entry is said to be "under the hand" of
the Master of the Company and/or one or both of the
Wardens. "Under the hand" means that the officials
mentioned signed something. Chambers suggests that
since there are never any signatures in the Register,
they must have been written in the book or manuscript concerned, and he quotes an entry which reads,
in part, "entred by commaundement from master
warden Newbery vnder his own handwrytinge on the
backside of ye wrytten copie." Greg, however, produces
convincing evidence for believing that this and other
cases cited by Chambers were exceptions and that the
normal practice was for the Warden to write and sign a
chit directing the clerk to make an entry. Occasionally
instead of "under the hand" we find "by authority" or
"by the warrant" of a Master or Warden, or "entered
for his copy by order of a Court."

The significant point about these references to the
signatures or authorizations of the chief officers of the
company is that each entry—each granting of a copyright—was a matter to be weighed by someone of experience and judgment, not merely a routine payment
of a fee and a routine entry made by the clerk. The entry in the Hall Book did not in itself confer copyright.
The copyright was conferred by the signed warrant of
one of the responsible officers. The entry made by the
clerk was the formal recording of the transaction.
When you buy a house it is true that the transaction is

not complete nor the title good until it has been entered by the county recorder; but it is not this recording which conveys title; this is accomplished by the
signing, sealing, and delivering.

Beginning in April 1607 another "hand" is mentioned almost every time a new play is entered:
namely, that of the Master of the Revels—at first Sir
George Buc, after 1623 Sir Henry Herbert.

3° October. [1610]
Walter Burre.   Entred for his Copy vnder thand*es* of
S*r* George Bucke & Th' wardens, a Comoedy called, The
Alchymist made by Ben: Iohnson.

It is very probable that the beginning of this practice in 1607 represents a successful attempt by the Master of the Revels to extend his licensing powers and
thus add to the office another source of fees. The whole
history of the Mastership of the Revels under Tilney,
Buc, and Herbert was one of steady pressure to consolidate and extend their licensing authority. But whatever the initial motive for the commencement of the
practice, it is safe to say that it had an effect upon the
establishment of the copyright of plays. For one thing
it removed the necessity of licenses from the ecclesiastical authorities: after 1607 we almost never find the
Bishop of London or his deputies mentioned as having
put their hands to any plays. The whole matter now
rested in the hands of a man experienced in theatrical
and dramatic affairs of every sort. Having licensed a
play for stage production, the Master of the Revels
would scarcely even have to reread it a year or two
later in order to license it for printing. Most impor-

tant of all, he was in a position, through his close contact with theater managers, to know about, and to be interested in, the ownership of a play manuscript. If a play, belonging, for example, to the King's Men, had been obtained surreptitiously, he would be likely to know or suspect this. At any rate the King's Men could easily—if they suspected such a thing—prevent publication—at least copyrighted publication—by a petition to the Master of the Revels. And we must assume that one of the points with which the Wardens of the Stationers' Company concerned themselves when considering an application for copyright was the applicant's legal right to the copy. An entry of 22 July 1598 in the Register reads

> **Iames Robertes.**/ Entred for his copie vnder the hand*es.* of bothe the wardens, a booke of the Marchaunt of Venyce . . . Prouided that yt bee not prynted by the said Iames Robert*es*; or anye other whatsoeuer wthout lycence first had from the Right honorable the lord Chamberlen.

This is a "staying entry" designed to prevent the publication of the play until the owners, the Lord Chamberlain's Men, were ready to release it. Such a matter would have been taken care of more or less automatically after 1607 when Buc established his authority over printed plays. That the concentration of the licensing of plays in the hands of one financially interested and technically competent was effective, is evident from the fact that after 1607 the number of plays printed surreptitiously drops off very noticeably. *King Lear,* 1608, will occur to many of you as a later

piracy, and of course there are others, but not so many
as before 1607.

The power of the Master of the Revels grew. Sir
Henry Herbert, Buc's successor, pressed his claim to
the licensing of all dramatic activities with such success that in 1630 his hand was considered necessary for
the printing of even a Latin academic play, *Ignora-
mus*.

But what of the men who wrote the plays? What
protection did they have? The copyright statute of
1710, as I pointed out, provided some protection for
authors. But in the early seventeenth century, when
copyright was in the hands of the Stationers' Company,
it existed for the benefit of the stationers, not of the
authors. When a dramatist sold a manuscript of a new
play, either to an acting company or to a publisher, he
sold it lock, stock, and barrel. Thereafter he possessed
no proprietary interest in it. He had disposed of the
copyright, which was inherent in the lawful ownership
of the manuscript. If the play later proved to be a failure, the author suffered only in his reputation. If it
became a popular success and was many times acted
"with great applause" or many times reprinted, only
the publisher profited directly. Indirectly, of course,
the copyright protection enjoyed by the publisher did
benefit the author, for without such protection no
publisher could have risked his money on a new book,
and the author would have been without a market
for his wares.

So far I have been speaking of original entries of
new books—of the establishing of copyright. It will be

well now to consider the transfer of assignment or copyright from stationer to stationer.

The earliest entries of assignment in the Stationers' Register are for the year 1577. For some years the clerk settled on no standard form for these, often scarcely distinguishing assignments from initial entries, and we have such formulas as the one of 1581 which I quoted earlier,

> Receaved of him for his licence to printe theis Copies hereafter mencõned.

Only as an afterthought—after a list of 43 titles—the clerk added

> wch were Sampson Awdeleys and nowe lycenced to the said Iohn Charlewood . . .

And this one of 13 August 1599:

> **Willm white** Entred for his copies . . . by assignem^t from Abell Ieffes. The spãnishe tragedie . . .

and again, 23 February 1599/1600—

> Entred and assigned ouer vnto humfrey Lownes from Iohn Busby . . .

Beginning in 1609 the form becomes pretty well standardized:

> **Iohn Wrighte/.** Assigned ou*er* to him from Thomas Busshell & wth Consent of m^r Adames war^d. vnder his hand . . . [13 September 1610]

Just as with initial entries, the authority of one or more of the officers is nearly always mentioned—"under the hands" is the usual phrase. Again something was signed by the Warden or Master—probably a note authorizing the clerk to make an entry in the Hall Book.

As time passes, the entries of assignments tend to become more explicit. No doubt this is the result of experience with inadequate records. About 1615, for example, we begin to find entries like this one of 9 April 1616:

> Assigned vnto the said Nicholas Bourne (at a full Court holden this day) by Katherin Rockett widowe as apeared by an assignem^t vnder her hand and seale, these 15 Copies that were heretofore entred to her husband Henrye Rockett deceased . . .

Or this one of 26 May 1623:

> **Felix. Kingston.** Assigned ouer to him by master man as appeareth by a note vnder his hand brought to this Court by his sonne Paule man, and Consent of the said Court, his part of RIDERS *Dictionary*.[5]

These two entries make it clear that the actual assignment of copyright was a private transaction between two stationers, effected by means of an instrument called an assignment, duly signed, sealed, and often, probably, witnessed. There is no reason to believe that this was anything new, it was only the mention of the document in the Register which was new. The transaction was entered in the Register merely as a matter of official record. As with initial entry, the clerk took no responsibility and required a warrant of approval from a full court or one or more of the officers. Unlike an initial claim of copyright, an assignment did not have to be recorded to be valid. As long as a claimant

[5] *Ibid.*, IV, 97.

could produce a satisfactory assignment, his ownership of a copyright, as of any other kind of property,
was secure. Another method of transfer, and a very
common one, was by legacy or inheritance. Katherine
Rockett, whose assignment to Nicholas Bourne I cited
a moment ago, had obtained her copies on the death of
her husband. Inheritance of copies, though often re-
ferred to later, is never itself recorded in the Register.
Unfortunately for the completeness of the record, entry in the Register was neglected about as often as it
was practiced. An early reference to a private transaction which was not properly recorded occurs in an
entry of 6 April 1579:

> **Miles Jennynges** Allowed vnto him *the historie of
> Gerillion* whiche he affyrmeth yat he bought of **Jhon
> Jugge.**[6]

Here the claimant seems to have lost the original assignment, if it ever existed, and had nothing to show
for it. On 4 July 1635 the following illuminating entry
was made:

> **M^r. Stansby.**   Entred for his Copies by vertue of a noate
> vnder the hand of Walter Burre & m^r Mathew Lownes
> warden bearing date the 10th of June 1621 as thereby
> appeareth these Copies following vizt./ by order of a
> Cort Euery Man in his humor The Silent Woman
> [and 5 other Jonson plays including *Cataline*].

Burre, the previous owner of these seven plays, disposed of them to Stansby in 1621, writing and signing
an informal assignment—a mere note. Stansby then
took this note to Stationers' Hall, where Warden

[6] *Ibid.*, II, 351.

Lownes signed his approval of the transaction. But Stansby did not bother to have it recorded—which would have put him to the expense of a sixpenny fee. Fourteen years later he still had the note in his possession; and when he learned that one I.S., probably John Spencer, was about to publish, or had already published, *Cataline,* he hastened down to Stationers' Hall to look at the Register and see what could be done about it. There he no doubt discovered, what Spencer had perhaps learnt earlier, that Burre had simply neglected the entering of *Cataline* before publishing it in 1611. Spencer's unauthorized publication then was, from a legal point of view, no piracy. When Stansby had bought the seven plays, he had thought that he was buying copyrights, but for *Cataline* none existed. When he discovered this fact, he presented to the Court his fourteen-year-old assignment from Burre and had it duly entered in the Register to make his title good. A comparable but even worse confusion [7] occurred in the copyright of *Epicene* (*The Silent Woman*) as a result of Stansby's failure to enter the assignment from Burre in 1621. In 1630 Burre's widow, finding evidence of her late husband's purchase of this play in 1612 but not finding in the Register any record of the assignment to Stansby in 1621 and hence concluding that it was a copy which she owned, proceeded to sell it to John Spencer. Thus both Stansby and Spencer had what each considered a clear title to the play. Since neither one subsequently

[7] I am indebted to Dr. Greg for bringing to my attention this additional illustration of my point.

printed the play and there is no further record of transfer, we do not know how, if at all, the difficulty was settled.

Having now examined the meaning of the wording of various kinds of entries in the Register, it will perhaps be instructive to take a specific play and reconstruct its early copyright history. For this purpose the *Merry Devil of Edmonton* will serve very well, since its record is fairly complete and normal. At some time in 1607 the bookseller Arthur Johnson obtained a manuscript of the play, which had belonged to the King's Men. How he acquired it we have, as usual, no way of knowing, but Johnson was a perfectly reputable member of the trade and there is no reason to suspect that he got it otherwise than honestly. Indeed the propriety of the transaction is in some measure vouched for by the fact that Johnson took the manuscript to Sir George Buc, who duly endorsed his name on the back of it or signed a separate memorandum licensing the printing of the play.[8] For this Johnson of course paid him a fee. His next step was to take the play manuscript and Buc's license to the wardens. At this point we are faced with a problem. How did

[8] Greg makes it clear, in "The Merry Devil of Edmonton," *The Library*, 4th Ser., XXV (1945), 122–39, that the MS could not have been the prompt copy. Otherwise it might reasonably be argued that Buc's hand—mentioned in Johnson's entry of 22 Oct. 1607 (quoted below)—was his earlier allowance for the acting of the play. Such however could not be the case, and I am driven to the conclusion, in spite of the short and corrupt text of Johnson's edition pointed out by Greg, that Buc's signature meant that Johnson had obtained it honestly and probably with the knowledge of the King's Men.

the wardens assure themselves that the book in question had not already been entered and copyrighted? They could not rely upon memory, since their term of office was but one year. Did they look back through the Register or ask the clerk to do this for them? Anyone who has ever searched for a book in the Register, not knowing the date, is well aware of the difficulties of this operation even when working with the neatly printed *Transcript*. That the stationers themselves sometimes experienced as great or greater trouble in finding book entries we have seen some evidence in the entry of *Doctor Faustus* in December 1592, previously quoted. And there are instances, though not so common as one might expect, of a book having been entered twice, apparently innocently. But it seems clear to me that the responsibility for finding out whether a book had been entered previously rested upon the applicant for a copyright. The Register was kept in the Hall for all members to consult, and I think they were expected to do it. If the clerk or the wardens themselves had been charged with this responsibility we may suppose that the task of searching through the book would have been made easier by some improvement in arrangement. A simple and rather obvious device, for example, would have been to set titles of books prominently in the left margin. Furthermore, stationers were frequently fined or required to make restitution when they had made the mistake of overlooking a lawful owner of a copyright. But we never hear of the clerk or a warden making a mistake of this sort. If anyone got into trouble it was the man who infringed a copyright by printing a book he had no right to. A warden, before approving an entry, doubtless exercised such care as he could to ascertain the facts—inquiring of the applicant whether he had searched the Register and how he obtained the copy—taking into consideration, we may suppose, the applicant's reputation for honest dealing. In difficult cases or when they were in doubt, the wardens apparently refused to act and left it to the full Court to decide at its next quarterly session. And there is one other point to consider. We have only the knowledge we can glean from imperfect records; the stationers themselves had the same records and perhaps more, and besides those they had much additional knowledge of a sort which is not recorded— knowledge which was simply in the air. The Stationers' Company was a guild—a closely knit organization of men all engaged in printing, buying, selling, and publishing books. They all knew each other and were in constant contact with one another, both socially and in their business relations. Of course they talked shop a great deal of the time, and it is reasonable to assume that they all knew most of the time what was afoot in the trade. It was quite possible, occasionally, for a printer to do a job on the sly; and mistakes were sometimes made; but gossip among apprentices and among masters kept every member of the trade fairly well informed of each man's activities. The master and wardens of the Company were always substantial men who had been in the trade for

many years. They would of course, by virtue of their
long experience and of their temporary official positions, be especially well informed.

But to return to Arthur Johnson, whom we left with
two wardens, seeking their approval for the entry of
his play in the Register. Very likely there was no difficulty about the *Merry Devil*. It was not a new play,
and the recent license from the Master of the Revels
supported the presumption, right or wrong, that the
King's Men had just released it for publication. And
Johnson was a man, so far as we know, of good reputation. So both the wardens signed a note directing
the clerk to enter it. Perhaps on the same day, possibly
within a few minutes, Johnson presented to the clerk
the manuscript and the chit from the wardens. The
clerk duly made the entry in the Register on folio
159 verso and collected his sixpenny fee:

> 22. Oct*ober*. [1607]
> **Ar***thur*. **Iohnson.**   Entred for his copie vnder thand*es* of
> Sr Geo. Buck k^t. and Thwardens. A Plaie called the
> Merry Devill of Edmonton   vj^d.

In 1608, or possibly toward the end of 1607, the first
edition of the play was published, with the imprint

> London/Printed by *Henry Ballard* for *Arthur Iohnson,*
> dwelling/at the signe of the white-horse in Paules
> Church/yard, ouer against the great North/doore of
> Paules. 1608.

Other editions printed for Johnson appeared in 1612
and 1617.

In 1624 Johnson began unloading his copyrights
in preparation for his return to his native Ireland,

and a bookseller named Francis Faulkner wanted two of them, including the *Merry Devil*. Presumably an instrument, formal or informal, was drawn up to effect this assignment. On or near June 21, Faulkner applied to George Cole, then one of the wardens. Again we do not know what steps Cole took to assure himself of the validity of Johnson's title, which had been transferred. But he was at any rate satisfied and signed an order directing the clerk to enter the assignment. Under date of 21 June 1624, accordingly, we find in the Register:

> **Fran: Faulkner**   Assigned ou*er* to him by Arthur Iohnson and order from m^r Cole warden all his estate in the 2 bookes following vizt The merry divell of Edmonton . . .   xij^d

With later editions and transfers we need not concern ourselves; they are all, apparently, perfectly regular.

Such was, in its main outlines, the system of copyright in the first half of the seventeenth century. Did it work? One kind of answer to this question may be arrived at by a few simple statistics. If I am right in saying that entry in the Register was a *sine qua non* of copyright, then many plays were never copyrighted. Of the fourteen plays (excluding masks) listed by Dr. Greg in his *Bibliography of the English Printed Drama* as first printed in the decade 1580 to 1589, six were not entered before or at the time of first publication; and of the twenty-five in the half decade 1610 to 1614 twelve were not entered—in each case one short of half. Of thirty-seven plays first printed in the 1590s, and of which more than one edition appeared before 1650, thirteen contain some flaw in copyright transfer; that is, we find them being published by someone who appears to have had no right to do so. Now some of the plays first published without entry and some of those published later without copyright were the result of culpable piracy; but most of such improper publications seem to have been the result of plain carelessness and incompleteness of the records when they ought to have been complete.

Mere figures, however, do not present a clear picture. We can throw better light on the workings of the system by looking at the whole copyright history of one play. The "Spanish Tragedy of Don Horatio and Bellimpera" was entered in the Stationers' Register on the 6th of October, 1592, to Abel Jeffes, duly approved by two of the ecclesiastical licensers. Jeffes had probably printed and published the first edition, a corrupt text, some months before the date of this entry and was led to make the entry only when he heard that Edward White was about to bring out a corrected text. But this step was ineffectual. White's edition, the first known, though undated, appeared at some time before December 18 of the same year, bearing on its title page the assertion that it was "Newly corrected and amended of such gross faults as passed in the first impression." Jeffes, not content to take this theft of such a valuable copyright lying down, appeared before the full court and demanded redress. His case as to *The Spanish Tragedy* was good, but there must have been a bitter fight, with accusations and counteraccusations, for on December 18 the court ordered that

> Whereas Edward white and abell Ieffes haue eche of them offendyd. viž Edw White in havinge printed the spanish tragedie belonging to Abell Ieffes/and Abell Ieffes in having printed the tragedie of arden of kent belonginge to Edw White. yt is agreed that all the book*es* of eche ympression shalbe as confiscated and forfayted, according to thordónnance, disposed to thuse of the poore of the companye. . . . And as touching their imprisonm^t for the said offenc*es* Yt is Referred ou*er* till some other convenient tyme. . . .

This must have cleared the air; at least it left Jeffes in full possession of his copyright, and he brought out another edition in 1594, which was, the imprint tells us, "Printed by Abel Jeffes and . . . sold by" none other than his erstwhile enemy, Edward White. The next steps are the transfer of the copyright from Jeffes to William White, Edward's son, in 1599, and the publication by the latter of another edition in the same year. In the following year, 1600, the well-known Pavier enters the picture—and the Stationers' Register:

> **Thomas Pavyer** Entred for his Copyes by direction of m^r white warden vnder his hand wrytinge: These Copyes followinge beinge thing*es* formerlye printed & sett over to the sayd Thoms Pavyer.

Then follows a list of twelve titles, six of them plays, including *The Spanish Tragedy*. This is a transfer, and though its language is strangely lacking in explicitness it seems to have been perfectly in order.

That there was no irregularity in the transfer of *The Spanish Tragedy* is well attested by the next three editions, 1602, 1603, and 1610, which were printed by William White, its previous owner, for Pavier. Incidentally, this William White was the warden who approved the transfer to Pavier. Pavier's title, then, appears to be perfectly clear. But in 1615, without any intervening record of a transfer, an edition is "Printed by W. White for J. White and T. Langley," and the next two, 1618 and 1623, are printed for Langley. What has become of Pavier? Was there an assignment from Pavier back to the White family which they never recorded? If so it is difficult to explain the next assignment which was recorded in August 1626, when the widow of Thomas Pavier transferred to Edward Brewster and Robert Bird sixty copyrights, including that of *The Spanish Tragedy*. The story is not quite finished yet: in 1633 the last edition of the seventeenth century was printed by Augustine Mathews for Thomas Grove, there being no recorded transfer to account for the imprint.

The Spanish Tragedy cannot be called typical in its copyright history. *Mucedorus,* for example, was printed seventeen times and owned by five men without a single hitch in its copyright or a single discernible gap in its record. But neither is *The Spanish Tragedy* by any means unique in the confusion and incompleteness of its copyright history. It is simply one of the best illustrations of the sort of thing which often happened, and an examination of the record supplied by Stationers' Register and imprints produces the impression that the system of copyright existing in the Stationers' Company was far from efficient. But I think this impression is not entirely accurate. On the whole it worked fairly well. We are apt to pay closer attention to the flaws in the system than to the smooth operation of it in plays like *Mucedorus*. And we must remember that the flaws which we see are very often flaws in the record rather than in the actual operation of the system: a copyright could change hands quite smoothly and quite securely without any entry being made in the Register. We must remember, too, that we are dealing with Elizabethans. The meticulous keeping of accounts and minutes, the systematic filing and cross-referencing and indexing, the careful preservation of records, as practiced today in government and business, are procedures developed by centuries of experience. The Elizabethans simply were not very systematic. Their systems of law enforcement and of finance, public and private, give ample proof of this. And the members of the Stationers' Company were undoubtedly well satisfied with a system of copyright which relied to a large degree upon common gossip, verbal agreements not recorded, and informal notes not preserved. Publishers thought they owned copyrights which they did not; they got into trouble over such mistakes and paid fines for them; they bickered and sued each other. But these difficulties were accepted philosophically as inescapable evidences of human imperfection. And through it all, literary property passed successfully from father to son and from husband to widow.

Appendixes

Supervising Committee, 1947

The English Institute

CONFERENCES

I. PROBLEMS IN TEXTUAL TRANSMISSION
SEPTEMBER 9–12, at 9:15 A.M.
Directed by HEREWARD T. PRICE, *University of Michigan*

A. The First Quarto of *Titus Andronicus*
HEREWARD T. PRICE, *University of Michigan*

B. Bad Quartos and the Unauthorized Edition of the *Religio Medici*
DONALD G. STILLMAN, *Bucknell University*

C. Problems in the Editing of Shakespeare
1. Text
MATTHIAS A. SHAABER, *University of Pennsylvania*
2. Interpretation
MATTHEW W. BLACK, *University of Pennsylvania*

D. Copyright of Plays in the Early Seventeenth Century
GILES E. DAWSON, *Folger Shakespeare Library*

II. MYTH AND LITERATURE
SEPTEMBER 9–12, at 10:45 A.M.
Directed by WILLIAM Y. TINDALL, *Columbia University*

A. Myth as Literature
RICHARD CHASE, *Connecticut College*

B. Mallarmé's *Hérodiade*
   WALLACE A. FOWLIE, *University of Chicago*

C. Myth, Concept and Poem
   PHILIP WHEELWRIGHT, *Dartmouth College*

D. The Modern Myth of the Modern Myth
   DONALD A. STAUFFER, *Princeon University*

III. PROBLEMS IN MODERN LEXICOGRAPHY
   SEPTEMBER 8–11, at 1:30 P.M.
   Directed by ATCHESON L. HENCH, *University of Virginia*

A. Problems Encountered in the Preparation of a Dictionary of American Words and Meanings
   M. M. MATHEWS, *University of Chicago Press*

B. Editing a Commercial Dictionary
   CLARENCE L. BARNHART, *Random House*

C. Collecting Current Vocabulary
   I. WILLIS RUSSELL, *University of Alabama*

D. The Capturing of Briticisms
   ALLEN WALKER READ, *Columbia University*

IV. THE THEORY OF FICTION
   SEPTEMBER 8–11, at 3:00 P.M.
   Directed by DAVID DAICHES, *Cornell University*

A. Attitudes to Fiction in the Eighteenth Century
   ERNEST BERNBAUM, *University of Illinois*

B. Sir Walter Scott
   DAVID DAICHES, *Cornell University*

C. George Eliot
   GORDON S. HAIGHT, *Yale University*

D. Aspects of Victorian Fiction
   E. K. BROWN, *University of Chicago*

   Note. The series on fiction will be continued in 1948.

EVENING MEETINGS

SEPTEMBER 8

Badness in Poetry

A discussion, with NORMAN HOLMES PEARSON,
Yale University, as moderator

SEPTEMBER 10

An Approach to the Poem
WILLIAM CARLOS WILLIAMS

Registrants, 1947

GELLERT S. ALLEMAN
Rutgers University

GEORGE ARMS
University of New Mexico

JOHN ARTHOS
University of Michigan

CLARENCE L. BARNHART
Random House, Inc.

JOSEPHINE BAUER
Columbia University

WARREN BECK
Lawrence College

ALICE R. BENSEN
Valparaiso University

ERNEST BERNBAUM
University of Illinois

JOHN P. BETHEL
G. & C. Merriam Co.

DOROTHY BETHURUM
Connecticut College

MATTHEW W. BLACK
University of Pennsylvania

WILLARD H. BONNER
University of Buffalo

FREDSON BOWERS
University of Virginia

ALICE S. BRANDENBURG
Wilson College

CLEANTH BROOKS
Yale University

ALAN W. BROWN
Columbia University

EDWARD K. BROWN
University of Chicago

MARGARET M. BRYANT
Brooklyn College

KATHERINE BURTON
Wheaton College

FRANK M. CALDIERO
Cooper Union

RICHARD V. CHASE
Connecticut College

STANLEY P. CHASE
Bowdoin College

JAMES L. CLIFFORD
Columbia University

MARJORIE D. COOGAN
Brooklyn College

KATHRYN COOK
Hobart College

THOMAS W. COPELAND
Yale University

CHARLOTTE E. CRAWFORD
Morgan State College

LUCILLE CRIGHTON
Gulfpark College

DAVID DAICHES
Cornell University

LEVETTE J. DAVIDSON
University of Denver

LLOYD J. DAVIDSON
University of Chicago

GILES E. DAWSON
Folger Shakespeare Library

CHARLOTTE D'EVELYN
Mount Holyoke College

ELLIOTT VAN KIRK DOBBIE
Columbia University

ALAN S. DOWNER
Princeton University

ELIZABETH DREW
Smith College

CHARLES KENNETH EVES
City College of New York

LAVINIA B. EVES
Hunter College

FRENCH R. FOGLE
Barnard College

STEPHEN F. FOGLE
University of Florida

FRANCES A. FOSTER
Vassar College

J. MILTON FRENCH
Rutgers University

WILLIAM FROST
Wesleyan University

ROBERT N. FULLER.
G. & C. Merriam Co.

KATHERINE HAYNES GATCH
Hunter College

GORDON S. HAIGHT
Yale University

AURELIA BROOKS HARLAN
Fort Collins, Colorado

J. LEE HARLAN
Fort Collins, Colorado

JULIA HARRIS
Meredith College

ALLEN T. HAZEN
University of Chicago

ATCHESON L. HENCH
University of Virginia

KATHERINE GEE HORNBEAK
Smith College

LISLE C. JOHN
Hunter College

CHARLES W. JONES
Cornell University

JOHN P. KIRBY
Mary Washington College

CLARA M. KIRK
Rutgers University

RUDOLF KIRK
Rutgers University

MARY E. KNAPP
Albertus Magnus College

EDWIN B. KNOWLES
Queens College

KATHRINE KOLLER
University of Rochester

FRANK A. KRUTZKE
Colorado College

JAMES CRAIG LADRIÈRE
Catholic University

STEPHEN A. LARRABEE
Waterville, Maine

LEWIS LEARY
Duke University

BENJAMIN LEASE
Illinois Institute of Technology

FRANCIS E. LITZ
Catholic University

LOUIS G. LOCKE
Southwestern University

CAROLINE S. LUTZ
*Westhampton College
University of Richmond*

THOMAS O. MABBOTT
Hunter College

ELIZABETH W. MANWARING
Wellesley College

MARY HATCH MARSHALL
Colby College

THOMAS F. MARSHALL, III
Western Maryland College

M. M. MATHEWS
University of Chicago Press

CHARLES A. MATZ, JR.
Rutgers University

C. WILLIAM MILLER
Temple University

FRANCIS E. MINEKA
Cornell University

LOUIE M. MINER
Brooklyn College

RUTH MOHL
Brooklyn College

JOHN F. MOORE
Connecticut College

LUELLA F. NORWOOD
Colby College

GERTRUDE NOYES
Connecticut College

ALBERT D. OSBORN
233 Broadway, New York City

JAMES M. OSBORN
Yale University

ALICE PARKER
Lindenwood College

WILLIAM R. PARKER
New York University

NORMAN HOLMES PEARSON
Yale University

HARRY WILLIAM PEDICORD
University of Pennsylvania

ABBIE FINDLAY POTTS
Rockford College

HEREWARD T. PRICE
University of Michigan

REV. CHARLES J. QUIRK, S.J.
Loyola University of the South

ALLEN WALKER READ
Columbia University

DAVID ALLAN ROBERTSON, JR.
Barnard College

H. BLAIR ROUSE
Ohio State University

I. WILLIS RUSSELL
University of Alabama

ROSEMARIE SCHAWLOW
University of Toronto

HELENE B. M. SCHNABEL
390 Wadsworth Avenue, New York City

MATTHIAS A. SHAABER
University of Pennsylvania

GEORGE SHERBURN
Harvard University

RAYMOND W. SHORT
Hofstra College

GEORGE L. SIXBEY
Centenary College

NATHAN C. STARR
Rollins College

DONALD A. STAUFFER
Princeton University

RUTH STAUFFER
Sarah Lawrence College

FREDERICK W. STERNFELD
Dartmouth College

HELEN L. STEVENS
Illinois Institute of Technology

DONALD G. STILLMAN
Bucknell University

RUTH Z. TEMPLE
Russell Sage College

DORIS THOMPSON
Russell Sage College

WILLARD THORP
Princeton University

WILLIAM Y. TINDALL
Columbia University

C. R. TRACY
University of Alberta

ROSEMOND TUVE
Connecticut College

EMMA V. UNGER
Carl H. Pforzheimer Library

HOWARD P. VINCENT
Illinois Institute of Technology

EUGENE M. WAITH
Yale University

CHARLES C. WALCUTT
Washington and Jefferson College

AILEEN WARD
Barnard College

HAROLD WENTWORTH
Temple University

PHILIP WHEELWRIGHT
Dartmouth College

J. EDWIN WHITESELL
University of South Carolina

AUTREY NELL WILEY
Texas State College for Women

MARGARET LEE WILEY
East Texas State College

EDNA R. WILLIAMS
Smith College

WILLIAM K. WIMSATT, JR.
Yale University

MARION WITT
Hunter College